EMBRACING CHAOS

EMBRACING CHAOS

STAVROS PAPAGIANNEAS

Cover design: Greta Cappellemans
Photograph of the author: Peter Loeffler

Published by STP Publications
Rue de la Science 14b
1040 Brussels
Belgium
Tel: +32 2 46084 00
email: sp@stpcommunications.com

ISBN: 978 94 6436 514 6

Too often we enjoy the comfort of opinion, without
the discomfort of thought.

— John F. Kennedy

Contents

Preface

Information comes to us at a speed far beyond what our brains can process. We are still mostly unaware of the impact of events on our daily lives. Even if you follow everything that happens, it remains challenging to remember what happened last month. Social media bombards us with little more than trivia, while outside that bubble, the world is experiencing a drastic shift in global power relations.

In December 2019, Greenpeace activists wrapped the EU Council building in images of fire and smoke in a striking protest intended to increase the pressure on European leaders to tackle climate change more ambitiously. The image is a classic representation of a dire predicament of our times: the EU is burning.

The Global South still views the EU as the Walhalla of the world, in which social welfare programmes get everyone into school and a straight set of teeth. Yet, the EU is far beyond that. With south–north migration at a historical peak, our current issues raise questions about human rights, warfare, and social and economic justice.

Crisis and austerity measures have been daily news since the Big Crash of 2008. By 2012, the crisis had rotted the very core of the European Union. The eurozone crisis indebted Greece, Portugal, Spain, Cyprus, and Ireland to the point that three supranational institutions had to intervene before anyone realised that national governments had lost sovereignty over their economies. The possibility of a Grexit was a nightmare for the EU.

Brexit was worse. The golden years espoused by Jim Morrison's famous line: "the West is the Best", have long gone. Things have worsened since 2012. In a referendum in 2016, the British decided they wanted a divorce from the woman they had never really loved but needed for all the financial and extra-legal advantages.

Over the last few years, climate change has become more urgent than ever. Climate activist Greta Thunberg became *Time*'s Person of the Year in 2019 and travelled around the world gathering support for her cause. And while Trump told her to chill, her contemporaries are anything but chilled.

A decade of pertinent crisis has resulted from governments powerless to resolve the issues of a polluting economy and controlling powerful transnational corporations. Detrimental industries such as biochemicals, weapons, and transport and resource exploitation preclude a highly positive vision of the future.

Climate change and human and animal extinction seem to be a direct consequence of the above. In a sense, it is a natural process that could reduce the likelihood of the Earth's survival. Natural laws do not provide for all species to continue to exist if an ecosystem is overpopulated. Species, including humans, will eventually disappear. Look at what has happened with the fires in Australia.

The start of 2020 saw grand predictions for the next decade, especially for the environment. Global advocacy groups have nicknamed it a "super year" for activism and action, highlighting the UN's Sustainable Development Goals (SDG) and the need to set a course for achieving the 2030 Agenda.

Adopted in 2015, the SDGs provide an international framework to move towards more equitable, peaceful, resilient, and prosperous societies by 2030 - while living within sustainable planetary boundaries.

Nevertheless, in March 2020, humanity woke up in a different universe. The outbreak of COVID-19 sent all the good predictions out of the window. The SDGs such as those on climate, the ocean, gender, life below water and on land, and responsible consumption and production will have to wait for their moment to shine.

Geopolitical tensions were already at worrying levels before the pandemic, but instead of uniting the world against this common enemy, the coronavirus crisis has demonstrated the fragility of our societies.

For centuries, epidemics have tested faith, friendships, and society. With the corona crisis, we are facing the most extensive global disaster of our generation. The coronavirus has already changed many things in our lives, and it will change global politics in profound ways. It is almost certain that a recession will strike the whole planet. The International Monetary Fund (IMF) predicts that the global economy will suffer its worst recession since the 1920s.

How will the world look once this crisis is under control? What will change on our planet and what will remain the same? It will take years for the significance to be fully understood. I believe that this crisis is a global turning point. There is a great deal of emotional, physical, and financial pain in the immediate future. However, a crisis of this scale will never be truly resolved until many of the fundamentals of our social and economic life have been changed.

One of the main things I have learned through this pandemic is that we are far more resilient than we think. It is incredible how people have kept their personal and work lives moving forwards by using innovative ways to stay socially connected. I believe that humanity will come out of this more agile and stronger.

Caring is part of our DNA. I saw many friends and stakeholders collaborating to support communities, whether creating masks and face shields or donating and delivering food to those in need. My company, StP Communications, launched an appeal in April 2020 to help alleviate the shortage of equipment in Brussels' residential care homes struggling to contain an increasing number of COVID-19 cases.

The current situation also entails the risk of widening social and economic differences around the world. Demand shifts and the capacity of the private sector to rebound will asymmetrically affect different countries. Many sectors are expected to suffer, notably through reduced turnover and employment.

This book is about Europe and its struggle to become a federation and reinforce its relations with the United States. Its determination to grow into a stronger geopolitical actor in an increasingly fragmented world, especially after four years of global disorder resulting from US President Donald Trump's activities.

The book is about contemporary and future challenges such as the corona pandemic, the identity crisis, the rise of populism, fake news, the new Cold War and why we need more regulation for online platforms, digital anarchy, global warming, and the rise of illiberal democracies. It is also about why our planet needs more empathy and compassion; about the need to develop laws to protect voters from fake news and propaganda such as those that are already in place for consumers. It is about why we should ask our politicians to take a political version of the Hippocratic Oath.

The pandemic has reminded European citizens of many things that they may have forgotten or taken for granted. We were reminded how linked EU economies are and how crucial a fully functioning single market is for our prosperity, and how we do things. The return of a more multilateral minded US under Joe Biden presents a new opportunity to consolidate the unification of the European continent and pursue more autonomous strategies.

The EU can now find US support in critical strategic issues such as those involving Russia, China, Turkey, and Iran. Take the essential steps necessary to achieve carbon neutrality by 2050 and to deepen the integration the embryonic Common Foreign and Security Policy (CFSP) needs to become a genuine common policy. A united Europe constitutes the only sustainable and viable future for the continent. Nevertheless, the European Union must change and adapt itself to the contemporary challenges with which it is currently faced. If it does not change, it will implode like the USSR.

Post Trump, Europe can further explore its relations with the US and even start building a future (con) federation – a Union of the West –together with the North Americans. The EU, the US, and Canada can build on the values they share such as the rule of law, human rights, and liberal democracy. The European Union is founded on respect for human dignity, freedom, democracy, equality, the rule of law and respect for human rights, including the rights of those in minority groups.

These values are common to its member states in a society where pluralism, non-discrimination, tolerance, justice, solidarity, and equality between women and men prevail. The historical relationship between the EU and the US is based on sharing and promoting the same values as those described above.

In the following chapters, I explore the challenges and opportunities for the next generations, seen through the glasses of a European communication scientist.

In the first chapter, I focus on the unprecedented changes that have been brought about by the global pandemic in the European Union, the United States, and beyond.

In Chapter 2, I try to uncover the deeper meaning of the corona crisis and speculate on the profundity of its consequences. I explain why our politicians should take a political version of the Hippocratic Oath.

Chapter 3 presents the lessons learned from the COVID-19 pandemic.

In Chapter 4, I "fast forward" through different types of populist electoral behaviour in Europe and America and analyse why today's citizens are voting for autocrats. I focus on the attempted coup at the Capitol and the birth of American fascism.

In Chapter 5, I focus on the slow process of unification of the European Union in an attempt to answer the question of whether "the EU is falling apart".

Chapter 6 assesses the demand for a profound change in the functioning of European institutions and the rise of pan-European parties such as Volt Europa and DiEM25.

In Chapter 7, I focus on the challenges for the European Union's sustainable future. More particularly, the chapter examines the opportunities of the upcoming Conference on the Future of Europe and includes recommendations.

Chapter 8 describes the identity crisis in Europe and its origins in nationalism and populism and examines EU bureaucracy and the division between North, South, and East.

Chapter 9 calculates the rise of illiberal democracies around the world focusing in particular on the cases of Hungary and Poland.

Chapter 10 describes the importance of communication in our daily lives. This chapter includes interviews with communication leaders and their opinions about what will change and what will stay the same after COVID-19.

Chapter 11 analyses the connected world of the future – the challenges and benefits. It is about how the world of technology leaves almost no aspect of life unchanged.

Chapters 12 and 13 monitor the battle against disinformation, fake news, propaganda, bots, trolls, and the dark side of the Internet. Here, the focus is on major public opinion manipulators like China, Russia, and Turkey and why we need more regulation for the Internet.

The objective of Chapters 14 and 15 is to evaluate the lessons learned from the Brexit campaigns and British nationalism.

In Chapters 16 and 17, I make the case for the future of EU–US relations after Trump. I present the critical importance of the creation of a future (con) federation between Europe and North America.

Stavros Papagianneas
Brussels – Corfu
March 2021

Chapter 1

A Brand New World

Honesty is the best policy, I will stick to that. The good shall have my hand and heart, but the bad neither foot nor fellowship. And in my mind, the main point of governing is to make a good beginning.

— Miguel de Cervantes

The book *La Peste* by Albert Camus published in 1947 reminds us that suffering is random. It is a story about an epidemic that spreads uncontrollably from animals to humans and destroys half the population of the town of Oran, in Algeria. When the city is quarantined, Doctor Bernard Rieux, the book's hero remarks: "From now on, it can be said that the plague is the concern of all of us".

For many, the world we live in today is as incomprehensible as the chemical composition of the geological layers underneath the soil we tread on. At a time where seventy years of European history is about to be turned around, it is increasingly difficult to get a firm grasp of what is happening on Earth.

Our planet needs more empathy and compassion. In the 1980s, long before the Internet changed how we do business, entertain ourselves, shop, travel, and the way we see and receive information, my first job was area manager for a large tour operator.

It was a good experience in managing staff, logistics, and operations in different countries. Can you remember what it was like travelling in the 80s or the price of a ticket? You could smoke on a plane, bring whatever you wanted, and security was not as it is today. You couldn't book tickets or hotels online.

Plane travel was an adventure. People dressed up for it, putting on their best clothes. Landing at your destination in one piece felt like a miracle and pilots were treated like demigods who needed thanks for their exceptional skills at bring us safely back to land. I clearly remember the times when plane travel happened without any electronic entertainment. Customs still existed then; luggage was checked and passports inspected.

Nowadays, in the coronavirus age, you are not allowed to travel, play sport, or go shopping. Hotels are closed and the aviation industry is grounded. Most European countries are in lockdown because of the outbreak. We are experiencing a triple crisis: medical, economic, and psychological.

I feel as if I'm in the film *Jeremiah Johnson*, the Western directed by Sydney Pollack starring Robert Redford, but rather in the flat country of Belgium. Jeremiah Johnson is a 70s movie about a man who turns his back on civilisation and learns a new code of survival in the brutal land of the isolated Rocky Mountains in the US.

With the corona drama, we are facing the most extensive global crisis of our generation. Our way of life and use of time has changed considerably due to shorter working hours, working from home, unemployment, and revaluation of time for ourselves. Do we feel free in that free time, and are we?

The coronavirus epidemic is a massive test for citizenship. As Yuval Noah Harari notes in his opinion piece in the *Financial Times* (March, 2020), humankind faces two particularly important choices. The first is between totalitarian surveillance and citizen empowerment. The second is between nationalist isolation and global solidarity.

In Europe, and around the world, governments are getting tougher, but what happens when restrictions slip? For example, Hungary proclaimed a state of emergency to deal with the situation, despite that all legal instruments were already at the government's disposal to take the necessary steps for controlling the epidemic. The parliament has been suspended. I don't believe that there was a need to declare a state of emergency.

The emergency law has triggered criticism from opposition parties, rights groups and the Council of Europe, because it does not set a specific limit on the time the additional powers will be in force. The draft legislation also creates new offences, for example anyone who publishes "false" or "distorted" facts could face up to five years in prison. With Orban's terrible track record on media freedom, this raises genuine fears that the law aims to crush Hungary's last critical voices.

On the other side of the world, Singapore measures proved to be effective but raised questions about the State's invasiveness. Surveillance cameras have helped the government find contacts of confirmed cases, who were then all quarantined.

Still, although needed, lockdown measures and unilateral closing of borders contradict not only the EU policies and goals on climate but also the fundamental freedom to provide services in the single market and the principle of free movement of workers.

COVID-19 will not only change global politics in profound ways but many things in our lives too. We are experiencing the most acute contraction in consumer spending ever and SMEs will need large state and EU funding to continue trading. We must join forces at the local, regional, national, European, and global level. It is almost certain that the international economy will suffer a massive recession, likely to be much bigger than that after the financial crisis of 2008-09.

The pandemic is a huge opportunity to show leadership and this especially in such a turbulent political period where citizens are no longer used to good governance. Nevertheless, the crisis needs to be addressed correctly and in a unified manner.

In Europe, there was a sluggish response to the pandemic and Italy criticised the EU for being slow to help when the first signs of the coronavirus epidemic appeared. There were even some signs of protectionism from some member states. The European Commission eventually restored order but even though the internal market was reopened their image was severely damaged. Italy, Spain, and Belgium were among the most affected countries. The panicked reactions of some European governments might have become new ammunition for those advocating protectionism. Voters will remember the news articles from countries snapping mouth masks and blocking protective aprons at the borders.

On 16 April 2020, the French President Macron warned of the collapse of the EU as a political project unless it supported stricken economies such as Italy and helped the country recover from the coronavirus pandemic. However, he added that the reflex of protectionism was fortunately corrected by a wave of European solidarity, such as COVID-19 patients from Alsace in France being admitted to intensive care units in German hospitals.

In other epidemics like Ebola and AIDS, the US led the world's response, but a more nationalist US is ceding leadership on this virus to China and Russia - even Cuba sent help to Italy. The total absence of Washington - under the Tump administration - is intriguing and brings into question American global leadership.

In contrast, UN chief Antonio Guterres has been giving wonderful lessons in leadership. On 19 March 2020, he called for world leaders to come together and provide an urgent and coordinated global response to this crisis. More than ever before, we need solidarity, hope, and the political will to see this through together, he said. A few days later, he called for an immediate global ceasefire in all corners of the world. Who would disagree? That is what our human family needs, now more than ever.

Our world is changing; both politically, socially, technologically, economically, and environmentally; and in our technology, education, health, eating and dress habits - there is hardly anything in life that is not changing. We like some of these changes while others create fear, anxiety, and feelings of insecurity.

Some of the changes are so fast and unexpected that it is hard to imagine how different everything was in the preceding years. The pandemic has accelerated the pace of this change and we are reorienting our relationship to government, to the outside world, and to each other. Despite the many government stimulus packages, the global economy has entered the opening stages of a recession that has the potential to become a depression. Also, the pandemic, intensified cold war II, at the same time revealing its existence to those who previously doubted it was happening.

The European illiberal union

In March 2017, the European Union celebrated the 60th anniversary of the signing of the Treaty of Rome, one of the most remarkable historical moments of the European integration process. It is utopian to believe that this momentum was an opportunity to save the European project or to reaffirm the commitment to a stronger and sustainable Union. A Union with the involvement of all the EU countries that share the wish to continue on the path to integration, based on the shared values and ideals of its founders.

The Union's fundamental values are respect for democracy, the rule of law, human dignity, human rights, freedom, and equality. These values unite all the member states. In principle, any country that does not recognise these values cannot join the Union. However, some member states do not respect these values and the dispute over the rule of law in some EU countries is damaging the European Union's global reputation and threatening its moral dignity and legitimacy. Many member states want to introduce new rules, allowing the EU to curb critical funding to those that violate the rule of law principles. Countries such as Hungary, Poland, Bulgaria, and Malta oppose that legislation. Hungary and Poland even vetoed the €1.8 trillion fund that was desperately needed for Europe's recovery from the coronavirus pandemic.

The stability of the Union is under threat by autocrats who are destroying the EU from the inside while receiving billions of euros from Brussels. The discussions with Poland and Hungary have not yet led these countries to realign with the EU's founding values. Members of the European Parliament were concerned about judicial independence, freedom of expression, corruption, the rights of minorities, and the state of affairs regarding migrants and refugees. In September 2018, Parliament demanded that the Council act to prevent the Hungarian authorities from breaching the EU's founding values.

In the case of Poland, the European Commission requested EU action in December 2017 in view of the perceived threats to the independence of the judiciary. In a resolution adopted in March 2018, the European Parliament agreed with the Commission on the risks to the rule of law in Poland.

In Bulgaria, anti-corruption protests against the government have been running since the middle of 2020. The state of the judiciary is one of the main causes of the demonstrations there, as protesters and opposition parties are increasingly making allegations that the prosecutor's office has been effectively captured by oligarchs using it for personal gain.

In addition, Malta, the smallest nation in the European Union, is earning a bad reputation, with a series of scandals involving allegations of bribery, cronyism, and money laundering. In 2017 Malta's most prominent journalist, Daphne Caruana Galizia, was brutally murdered as she drove from her home not far from the country's capital, Valletta. She was known simply as "Daphne", and had spent years covering corruption at the highest level of Maltese government and society on her widely-read blog, "Running Commentary".

The Brexit disaster

In June 2016, the United Kingdom left the EU after a referendum based on lies and manipulation of the public opinion by right-wing extremists of the UKIP (UK Independent Party) and political opportunists like Boris Johnson. The UK voted to leave the EU and officially left the Union - it's nearest and most significant trading partner - on 31 January 2020. However, both sides agreed to keep many things the same until 31 December 2020, to allow enough time to agree to the terms of a new trade deal. It was a complex and bitter negotiation, but a deal was finally agreed on 24 December.

Brexit has been brewing in the UK's Conservative party for more than 30 years. In 1988, Margaret Thatcher delivered a legendary speech in Bruges that can be considered as the launch of modern Tory Euroscepticism. She believed that the vision of Social Europe - in the meantime, one of the major EU achievements - was a bridge too far. She warned of the concentration of power "at the centre of a European conglomerate". Her most controversial statement still stands as one of the basic credos of Brexiteers: "We have not successfully rolled back the frontiers of the state in Britain only to see them reimposed at European level, with a European superstate exercising a new dominance from Brussels".

A few days before, Jacques Delors, the President of the European Commission, had told the Trades Union Congress that Britain's labour movement should embrace a "uniquely European model of society" and support the Commission in building a "platform of guaranteed social rights". Thatcher was afraid that European law would strengthen the power of the unions, after almost ten years of a Conservative government in Britain battling to reduce it.

Still, leaving the EU brings high economic and political costs. It will reduce the UK's standing in the world and its ability to influence the international events that affect it the most. Brexit will be remembered as a gigantic mistake of British conservatives determined to push Britain out of the EU. The effects will be felt sharply in the short term and have a lasting impact on the UK and the EU for many years to come. Britain's exit of the EU has only losers and will cause a slow motion implosion in the United Kingdom. The Scottish National Party is pushing for a second referendum on Scottish independence and Wales and Northern Ireland are dissatisfied too. The support for a united Ireland will increase if there ended up being a hard border between the Republic of Ireland and Northern Ireland. Leaving the EU would be calamitous for the economy of those parts of the UK. In Scotland, in particular the support for its ability to take its own decisions as an independent country will only grow further.

Worst outcome of US leadership

In the US, democracy is vanishing. Following the rioting at the Capitol on 6 January 2021, America has lost its status as a democratic example in the world. "This was a coup attempt," said historian Anne Applebaum, author of *Twilight of Democracy: The Seductive Lure of Authoritarianism*. In the book, which is on Obama's list of favourite books from 2020, she grapples with why so many of her contemporaries across the globe have abandoned liberal democracy in favour of strongman cults and autocratic regimes.

The entire planet was astonished that day, as armed supporters of US President Donald Trump stormed the Capitol building in Washington in an effort to stop lawmakers from confirming President-elect Joe Biden's electoral win –usually a ceremonial event.

Driven by Donald Trump's false claims that the election had been stolen from him, when he actually lost to Joe Biden by seven million votes, supporters came from all over the country to listen for a last time to their president. And when he asked them to they marched up to the Capitol Hill, believing that they were doing something patriotic. Five people died.

Kellyanne Conway, President Trump's senior adviser, said in August 2020 while resigning, that the US president stood to benefit politically from the kind of unrest that had erupted that month in Kenosha, Wisconsin, after the police shooting of an unarmed Black man, Jacob Blake. "The more chaos and anarchy and vandalism and violence reigns, the better it is for the very clear choice on who's best on public safety and law and order," Conway said on *Fox & Friends*.

The greatest weapon of the US has always been the power of the democratic example. After World War II, countries wanted to be like America, with its freedom, prosperity, and two and a half centuries of nonviolent transfer of power. It was, together with the European Union, a useful driver of the spread of democracy around the world.

These days the United States, torn apart by insurrection, and mass misinformation, is witnessing a political and social realignment. The Republican Party might split, starting with the relatively small movement of the "Never Trumpers" breaking off in 2016 and joined four years later by a new group of establishment Republicans repulsed by Trump's post-election actions.

America's opponents did not miss the opportunity. The Chinese Foreign Ministry drew parallels with the protests in Hong Kong, where there were no casualties and Moscow found the US political system "outdated". Iranian President Hassan Rouhani called the US a "fragile and weak Western sub-democracy".

Corona, climate change, Black Lives Matter: all of these are challenging and Herculean tasks for Joe Biden to fulfil. Yet, he could set the trend for American politics for the decades to come. He would be an unexpected hero if he succeeds, and an easy target if he fails.

Chapter 2

Don't Panic

If I do not violate this oath, may I enjoy life, and art, respected while I live, and be remembered with affection thereafter. May I always act so as to preserve the finest traditions of my calling and may I long experience the joy of healing those who seek my help.

— Hippocratic Oath

At the beginning of March 2020, my inbox was a mix of people cancelling meetings and events. "The EU faces a 'moderate to high' risk of 'widespread sustained transmission' of the coronavirus," the European Centre for Disease Prevention and Control said on Monday 2 March 2020. They told us that COVID-19 is no ordinary flu. It is not seasonal influenza of the type that affects many people every winter. Research so far indicates that the coronavirus spreads more rapidly and has a much higher death rate than the flu. Panic took over and panic is often not a good adviser.

Over the past few decades, neuroscientists have shed new light on how chronic stress can make the brain more susceptible to mental health disorders. Many of these studies have looked at the long-term effects of adverse childhood events (ACEs) or living through traumatic events like terrorist attacks. The majority have shown that there are some who display more resilience when faced with this type of challenge and that resilience is an active neurobiological process that can protect the brain despite increased and prolonged stress.

With the rapid spread of the pandemic, people around the world expressed panic through various behaviours which have affected economies, social values, and caused stress to those involved regardless of the directness of contact with the infected.

In her book *Pandemics* published in 2007, Debra Miller argues that a vast number of people being affected in such a short period overwhelms countries, resulting in them being unable to provide health care, maintain the society of their community, or keep the economy functioning. This could disrupt the world economy with declining stock markets, scarcity of supplies, worsening political instability, and governments losing billions in revenue.

Media communication may appear to be accurate and effective at informing the public. However, it can also misinform and contribute to unnecessary public panic resulting in undesirable responses. Governments need to develop communication strategies and specific messages that can effectively convey desired information at different stages of the anticipated pandemic.

Marijn De Bruyn, Professor of Health Psychology and currently working at the Corona Behavioural Unit at the Dutch National Institute of Public Health and the Environment (RIVM), believes that the most substantial difficulty for public communicators during the pandemic is "the relentless speed of changes in policies, the very short turnaround between decisions regarding new measures and the press conferences".

He added that the three main communication actions that work efficiently are:

(a) being very explicit and clear about behavioural recommendations for citizens;
(b) communicating urgency and effectiveness of measures to support motivation; and
(c) acknowledging difficulty and efforts by citizens and organisations.

Stefano Rolando is a Professor of the IULM University Milano and President of the Club of Venice – an informal group of the most senior communications professionals from EU member states' governments, candidate countries, and European institutions. In an interview, he stated that the most substantial difficulty for public communicators during the pandemic was that they "have to be loyal to the institutions while also producing social and cognitive values for the citizens. They are not officials. They are mediators. Therefore, they must be aware of both the increasing functional illiteracy and of the way in which the digital divide takes a bigger toll on the more fragile ones".

"They must refuse the systematic practice of propaganda of which the counter-side is exclusion. In situations of crisis, the first phase consists of regulating social and collective behaviour. This phase is relatively easy. Afterwards, it is necessary to generate a process of responsibilisation in order to trigger a solidarity recovery and a constructive debate between society and the institutions. Here, the propaganda-like systems don't give any space to those who think that communication is the most critical explanation," he added.

As of writing, there are already around 390 million confirmed cases and approximately 3.8 million deaths according to the Johns Hopkins University Coronavirus Resource Center.

The Organisation for Economic Co-operation and Development (OECD), which represents the 36 most advanced economies on the planet, urged governments worldwide to cooperate more closely, calling for an international response as the virus spreads. In 2020, it warned that an escalation in the coronavirus outbreak could cut global economic growth in half and plunge several countries into recession.

Most cities in the world are in lockdown. We see travel restrictions in place and closures of companies mounting. Global trade, commerce, tourism, investment, and supply chains seem to be in disarray. It's clearly not a good time to be in the automotive industry or in the travel and tourism business. Tourism-dependent countries are struggling economically as fearful tourists decide to postpone their holidays. Just how bad could it get? However, whether the economy slides into recession would be determined by the way businesses react to the outbreak. The age of hysteria is upon us, but let's never forget that it is the cool, calm, and wise minds that will find future pathways and embrace sustainable solutions. To reduce the disruption caused by the coronavirus outbreak to an acceptable level, organisations should implement a crisis plan by combining preventative and recovery measures.

They should also prepare for the post-crisis as did Hong Kong in 2003 with the SARS (Severe Acute Respiratory Syndrome) outbreak. Also a coronavirus, SARS differed from previous epidemic infectious diseases in its explosive spread, which caught the health and hospital authorities by surprise. SARS killed only a few thousand, according to official statistics. During the outbreak, the city was perceived as the centre of the global fight against the virus with serious consequences for local business and tourism. While the international focus was on fighting SARS, Hong Kong authorities and the private sector joined forces to prepare the post-crisis phase, promote economic recovery, and prepare a post-SARS return to economic growth.

Hong Kong authorities committed USD129 million (€100 million) to a programme seeking to:

(a) promote local and international confidence in Hong Kong;
(b) promote business, tourism and local production; and
(c) attract international business.

They created an international communications plan for supporting the three objectives mentioned above. The plan turned out to be very successful in restoring the international community's confidence and in promoting economic recovery after the elimination of the virus.

The SARS outbreak, which reached 29 countries, was ultimately contained using traditional public health measures, such as testing, isolating patients and screening people at airports, train stations, and other public places where they might spread the virus. There was enormous panic just as there is now. COVID-19 will also disappear soon and like SARS will become a case study. The press will publish articles about lessons learned from the corona hysteria and how social media contributed to this. Don't forget – there was neither Facebook, Twitter, nor Instagram in 2003.

The coronavirus is an opportunity to show leadership, especially in a turbulent political period in which citizens are no longer used to it. Nonetheless, the condition is that the crisis should be tackled properly and with unity.

With the corona outbreak, we are facing the most extensive global crisis since WWII. According to the UN's environment chief, Inger Andersen, nature is sending us a message with the pandemic and the ongoing climate crisis. Andersen stated that humanity is placing too many pressures on nature with damaging consequences and warned that failing to take care of the planet meant not taking care of ourselves.

More than ever, we have to be innovative and creative to manage this situation in many sectors. Leaders of private or public organisations need to brace themselves for the scenarios that may play out in their associations due to the consequences of the spread of the virus. The challenges for establishments in affected countries include infected staff, a drop in activity, disruption in global supply chains, decreased travel, cancelled events, and companies forced to close. Stakeholders need to know how organisations intend to navigate the crisis.

The outbreak of the coronavirus has led to disinformation that obstructs efforts to contain the disease. We hear fake news that the Schengen Area has collapsed or that EU countries are fighting each other for decreasing supplies of medical equipment, etc. With the crisis in full progress, the spread of misinformation could lead to fear and distrust unless businesses and associations communicate effectively and demonstrate their preparedness to deal with the situation. The World Health Organization (WHO) has said that fake news is spreading faster than the virus and has named it an "infodemic of planetary proportions". The outbreak has also provoked social stigma and discriminatory behaviour against citizens of specific ethnic backgrounds and anyone perceived to have been in contact with the virus.

Governments, institutions, and corporations need to constantly reinforce public trust and enhance their reputation via their communications on successfully managing the rising complications of this global crisis.

The death of a gerontologist

In October 2020, Dimitris Kampanaros committed suicide. He was the owner of a nursing home in the northern Athens suburb of Agios Stefanos.

A few days before his desperate act, as well as himself, two residents of the home had tested positive for COVID-19.

Dimitris Kampanaros was very dedicated to his work and had an immense sense of duty and respect for his residents. Katerina, an old friend from the Italian School in Athens, told me that she had been in contact with him on behalf of her mother and that he was an exceptional person.

When the pandemic broke out in March 2020, the gerontologist took the initiative to stay inside the building for 65 days together with the residents and his staff. Although Athens has successfully managed the first corona wave things are now more difficult. Greece entered the second wave of the pandemic in August of the same year, and the health system is feeling the pressure of the gradual increase in incubated patients – this is the same situation in many EU countries.

When EU leaders held an informal video conference on 29 October 2020 to discuss the unfolding pandemic disaster, the possibility of another lockdown was on the agenda. As efforts to limit the spread with soft methods didn't seem to work in overpopulated areas, a new lockdown was a radical step that nobody wanted.

A slow economic rebound is already losing steam, and the social backlash against the latest restrictions is gathering momentum. There is pressure to devise something coming close to a coherent EU response. Unanimity has always been Europe's worst enemy.

The planet is beset by enormous problems that defy political and healthcare boundaries. Doctors and healthcare staff are fighting a global war against a pandemic that could have been prevented. Nevertheless, although the reports and the alarming scenarios were there, the budget, the long-term planning, and the cooperation were not.

Certain members of the dominant political class are more concerned about the number of votes than the well-being of the citizens. Look to Boris Johnson or former US president, Donald Trump. There is also the type of autocrat like Erdogan or Bolsonaro elected through manipulation of public opinion, lies, or strategic marketing promoting imaginary enemies. For them, domestic problems are always brought in from the outside, never from within the country itself.

Politics is not about staying in power whatever it takes. It is about managing the state for the people and by the people. It is about what you can do for the village, the city, the country, the continent, and the world. It is not about how to become rich. It is about caring, respecting, being empathetic, and having compassion. It is about taking difficult decisions, being transparent, communicating well, and being proactive.

One of the oldest binding documents in history – the Oath of Hippocrates – is still held sacred by physicians: to treat the ill to the best of one's ability, to preserve a patient's privacy, to teach the secrets of medicine to the next generation. This oath of ethics is one of the most widely known Greek medical texts.

There are still many things that we need to do to save humanity and the planet. But what if we required our politicians to take a political version of the Hippocratic Oath? After all, when we elect a government, we are entrusting the health of politics to their hands.

Translating the Hippocratic Oath from medicine to politics is easy. You don't have to change a single word.

For example, with the modern version, a physician vows, among other things, that:

> *If I do not violate this oath, may I enjoy life, and art, respected while I live, and be remembered with affection thereafter. May I always*

act so as to preserve the finest traditions of my calling and may I long experience the joy of healing those who seek my help.

All of us, including politicians, have to focus on what we do every day with an eye on future generations. We should ask ourselves if we are acting in "the finest traditions" of our vocations and will know "the joy of healing" those who seek our help.

Chapter 3

Lessons Learned from the Corona Crisis

A perfect storm takes place when a rare combination of disparate circumstances produces an event of extreme violence: in such case, a synergy of forces releases energy much greater than the mere sum of its individual contributors.

— Slavoj Zizek

All that was considered normal before the corona crisis – the "previous normal" of January 2020 – is gone. Forever. Investing now in building an innovative and sustainable strategy to come out of recession is of prime importance. Embrace the new normal and drive innovation into every aspect of organisations to exit recession on a growth trajectory.

However, some things will return to the previous rhythms after mass vaccination. We have missed the regularity of going to the restaurant, visiting friends, going on holidays, the football match, etc. One of the things that will undoubtedly remain is what we do now. We can do one-third - or more - of our work from home. The way we work has changed. But even if the virus becomes endemic and we need to be vaccinated annually, I am not sure that we will go back to warring masks and social distance unless there is a really dangerous outbreak.

After the appearance of AIDS, and despite the fact that HIV was a dangerous virus, people continued to have unsafe sex, so now many will return to their unsafe social habits because we are too social for insisting on distances.

For the past year, our planet has been mired in a deep crisis with tremendous health, economic, social and political dimensions. I believe we are living amid the first global mass trauma event for several decades to come. It is probably the first of its kind since World War II and likely the first of such severity in our lifetime. What we have learned over the past 12 months could pay off for years to come.

Combating myths

The 2020 coronavirus has given rise to a tsunami of conspiracy theories, disinformation, fake news, and propaganda, eroding public trust and undermining health officials. It can also lead to a significant crisis, panic, and hysteria. We saw many claims that the "virus is a foreign biological weapon"; that the virus has been "created in NATO laboratories", or it is a "partisan invention", or part of a "plot to re-engineer the population".

According to the WHO, disinformation related to the pandemic is just as dangerous as the virus itself. False preventative measures hinder the fight against illness, such as:

(a) traditional African treatments; and
(b) fake remedies, like eating garlic, drinking warm water with lemon slices or alcohol.

The WHO has created a particular page on its site to debunk myths about the pandemic and the United Nations has developed the global Pause campaign #takecarebeforeyoushare, which consists of videos, graphics, and colourful gifs that stress sharing only trusted and accurate science-based social media content.

There is a predominant element here that we must consider. We have faced pandemics before, but it is the very first time the world faces an epidemic at a time when humans are as connected and have as much access to information as they do now. According to a report of the European External Action Service's (EEAS) special team dedicated to highlighting such digital tactics, China used the global coronavirus crisis to spread false reports and other online disinformation. The EEAS said that more than 150 cases of pro-Kremlin disinformation have been linked to the global health crisis since late January 2020. That includes claims that the European Union was at the point of collapse because of national governments' slow response to the crisis.

"Those spreading disinformation harm you," European Commission President Ursula von der Leyen said in an online video statement. The European Commission has also launched a dedicated Coronavirus response website that provides real-time information on the virus and the EU response. Fact-checking and academic communities supported by the EU have stepped up their efforts.

The European Commission and the EEAS have been in contact with all major social media platforms to increase the promotion of authoritative content, take decisive action on false or misleading content – that could cause serious harm – and take down illegal content. According to the European Commission, social platforms have escalated their response to tackle disinformation:

- Since the outbreak of the crisis, Twitter has seen a 45% increase in usage of Twitter Moments – curated content that allows for global coronavirus tracking.
- Facebook and Instagram Info hubs have directed more than 2 billion people to resources from health authorities, including the World Health Organization (WHO).
- YouTube has reviewed over 100,000 videos related to dangerous or misleading coronavirus information and has removed over 15,000 of them.

The Commission urged companies to share relevant data with the research and fact-checking community and work together with authorities in all member states.

By 29 April 2020, the services of the European Commission had identified 2,700 articles daily containing coronavirus-related potential disinformation. Online platforms report millions of false or misleading posts, which shows massive potential for disinformation to flourish. The crisis has opened the door to new risks for citizens to be exploited or become victims of criminal practices in addition to targeted disinformation campaigns by foreign and domestic actors seeking to undermine EU democracies and the credibility of the EU and its member states.

One of the most incredible myths is a conspiracy theory linking the spread of the coronavirus to 5G wireless technology. There were more than 100 incidents in April 2020 alone in Belgium, the Netherlands, and the UK of the destruction of 5G infrastructure, such as masts and cabins. Premised on this false idea – which has gained momentum in Facebook groups, WhatsApp messages, and YouTube videos – radio waves sent by 5G technology are causing small changes to people's bodies that make them succumb to the virus.

Many people have noticed that Wuhan was very advanced on the 5G rollout and suspected a possible link with the coronavirus outbreak in that region. However, the coronavirus has also spread in many countries that do not have 5G installations. Claims that COVID-19 originated in Wuhan due to China's 5G network are unfounded and dangerous. Many platforms, including the EU-funded SOMA project and its network of fact-checkers, have debunked these conspiracy theories.

On 10 June 2020, China and Russia have once more been accused by the European Union of running disinformation campaigns inside the EU.

> "Foreign actors and certain third countries, in particular Russia, and China, have engaged in targeted influence operations and disinformation campaigns around COVID-19 in the EU, its neighbourhood, and globally, seeking to undermine democratic debate and exacerbate social polarisation, and improve their own image in the COVID-19 context," a communication of the European Commission states.

In March 2021, Gideon Rachman, chief foreign affairs commentator for the Financial Times, described the ongoing Korean conflict, China's military moves targeting Taiwan, Chinese Wolf warrior diplomacy, Western condemnation of the Uyghur genocide and Alexey Navalny's imprisonment, and Russian-Western tensions over Ukraine as proof that the new cold war is happening or close to happening. Russia and China pose a significant cyber warfare threat.

Why does misinformation flourish? Does all this fake news mean that people are extremely trustful, their anxiety making them receptive to the most flagrant rubbish? While many share fake news for fun, fake news about potential corona cures has been the most worrying during the past months.

The manipulation of information represents a huge risk that might have catastrophic effects on societies, triggering possible conflicts, and creating further tensions among people and different communities. Fabricated information increases discrimination and creates religious, ethnic, and political divisions and encourages hate speech.

Information freedom is paramount

Freedom of expression and media and information freedom are crucial for the functioning of a democratic society and continue to be so in times of crisis. Providing correct information about public health risks fast is an essential element of crisis management.

Media play a key role with increased responsibility not only in the provision of accurate, reliable information to the public but also in the prevention of panic and fostering people's understanding for and cooperation with necessary restrictions. Media organisations and journalists should uphold the highest professional and ethical standards. They should prioritise authoritative messages regarding the crisis and refrain from publishing, and thus amplifying, unverified stories.

Governments and institutions should regularly and promptly inform the public about the dimensions and implications of the crisis and governments' measures. They should engage in open communication that promotes trust and cooperation with every individual. However, the flow of information about the pandemic should not be reduced to official communications as this would lead to censorship and suppression of people's concerns.

Media, medical staff, civil society, and the general public should have the right to criticise the authorities in their response to the crisis. This is particularly important when other checks and balances on government action are removed or eased, especially under emergency measures, or even a state of emergency in some countries. The story of Doctor Li Wenliang, the Chinese whistleblower, who was trying to alert fellow medical professionals to alarming symptoms, shows the dangers of suppressing the free flow of information.

According to Foreign Policy – reporting about the situation in the US–the PeaceHealth St. Joseph Medical Center in Bellingham, Washington, fired Doctor Ming Lin after he posted on Facebook about gaps in protective equipment and precautions. The *New York Times* has reported that Doctor Deena Elkafrawi was censored by the Lincoln Medical and Mental Health Center in the Bronx after being quoted in print saying she feared going to work. Even New York University's Langone Medical Center warned its doctors that they could be fired if they spoke to the press.

US President Donald Trump's daily spectacle of calling journalists horrible and incompetent and denigrating their credentials is hardly new. However, it intensified with Trump visiting the podium daily and insulting those who raised topics he would rather not confront.

Professional journalists' role in covering the pandemic was vital in light of Trump's persistence at spreading misinformation. Threatening and insulting journalists have emboldened and inspired leaders globally including Trump himself in his criticism of the media. His practices were a real danger for the right to information, a cornerstone of our democratic societies.

In Russia, Doctor Anastasia Vasilyeva, the head of a medical trade union, accused President Putin of lying about the coronavirus. Through the union's website and social media, she has exposed false government assurances that the health system is coping and frontline health workers are well protected from the infectious virus. Authorities reacted with fury to her criticism and arrested her. Months ago, as the coronavirus started to spread worldwide, the Kremlin insisted that Russia would be fine. The

Russian President dismissed reports of an epidemic as fake news spread by foreign enemies.

Using the epidemic as an excuse to silence critics or political opponents is a practice that should be avoided. Emergencies have been used many times in the past as justifications for curbing free speech. However, fake news does not only target political organisations and policymakers.

Digital will set you free

Never in the past has digital connectivity been so critical for a health crisis. The coronavirus pandemic has made us realise how heavily we depend on digital connectivity. The public is far more engaged and has more exacting and higher expectations.

In the Digital 2020 April Global Statshot Report, we find a detailed analysis of how people around the world are using the Internet, social media, mobile devices, and e-commerce.

Key headlines in this report include:

- Big jumps in digital activity, especially in countries that have seen the strictest lockdowns.
- Significant increases in social media use, with video calling taking centre stage.
- Accelerating adoption of e-commerce, particularly for grocery shopping.
- An increase in the amount of time spent playing video games and watching sport.

This is an opportunity for public and private organisations to reinforce public trust and reputation. They can learn how to be better prepared to manage rising complications of a global crisis, respond to it much faster, and adjust their action and message to align with the public good.

Empathy, authenticity, humanity, ethics, and connectivity are the new success

More than two millennia ago the Greek philosopher Socrates famously said that humility is the greatest of the virtues. His timeless observation was that the wisest people are the first to admit how little they know. In the last decade scientists have offered many new studies examining this characteristic and its effects on our thinking and reasoning. According to this research, people with greater humility are better learners, decision-makers, and problem solvers. Humble people make the most significant leaders and the best communicators.

I firmly believe that the coronavirus is a good opportunity for brands to change attitude and reach out to people, not clients, or consumers. Putting people above budgets and profits is very important. There is no doubt that companies are facing a substantial decline in revenue, but pushing sales at this time would be ineffective and even opportunistic. So, companies should play the long-term game and invest in trust and reputation. It is time to learn how to create community values and principal focus points.

This crisis should create a new culture of ethics. It is crucial that governments, citizens, and private and public organisations consciously create the kind of urgent ethics that are reasonable, transparent, fair, and broadly agreed by everyone. There is a big difference in ethics between Dominic Cummings, the (former) communication guru of the UK's prime minister Boris Johnson and Prime Minister Mark Rutte of the Netherlands. Rutte did not visit his dying mother because of the coronavirus restrictions, while Johnson's most senior adviser, said that he acted reasonably and legally after driving 418 km from his home to Durham during lockdown.

There is a big difference between the PM of New Zealand, Jacinda Ardern, and US President Donald Trump. In a crisis, leaders need to explain what is happening. Arden is a brilliant example of leadership and knows that empathy is crucial. She also knows that this is not enough when people's heads are spinning. Her messages are clear, consistent, and somehow simultaneously sobering, and have a calming effect. Her approach does not just resonate with her countrymen on an emotional level. It is also working remarkably well.

That is quite the opposite of the style of Donald Trump. He claimed that he would use his entire presidential prerogative to ensure violent protests end in the wake of the demonstrations resulting from the murder of George Floyd. He threatened to deploy "thousands and thousands of heavily armed soldiers, military personnel and law enforcement officers" to bring order. No empathy, no humanity, no ethics, and no connectivity. Trump tried to divert attention from his failed approach concerning the corona crisis. He sought to steer conversations in a different direction and appealed to his most extreme supporters. He created imaginary enemies: the so-called alt-left – in this context, all those against police brutality.

Another charismatic leader who knows how to reassure citizens in times of crisis and influence is Justin Trudeau, Canada's PM. Trudeau's very long pause after being asked about the George Floyd protests in the US speaks volumes louder than his actual response. It is a very political and diplomatic response by answering something different from what was asked. This is what happened during a press conference on the front steps of Rideau Cottage in Ottawa on 2 June 2020. The Canadian prime minister was asked for his thoughts on US President Donald Trump's call for military action against protesters. After 20 seconds of silence, Trudeau finally spoke:

> "We all watch in horror and consternation what's going on in the United States."

"It is a time to pull people together, but it is a time to listen, it is a time to learn what injustices continue despite progress over years and decades."

And he stressed: "It is a time for us as Canadians to recognise that we too have our challenges, that Black Canadians face discrimination as a lived reality every single day."

Social media must embrace transparency and ethics

The lessons learned from governments and citizens' different actions across the planet against the spread of disinformation and racist content on social media platforms is that people have had enough. Not only international organisations and governments but also private companies are taking measures to bring order to the malicious chaos created by these platforms in citizens' daily lives.

There is a tremendous global demand for more social responsibility and transparency and less racism, intolerance, and hate speech. In June 2020, Coca Cola, Unilever, Honda, and Levi Strauss stopped advertising on Facebook, Instagram, and Twitter in a boycott over racist content. In particular, Facebook faces a growing boycott by advertisers unhappy with its handling of misinformation and hate speech.

COVID-19 has not only caused unprecedented damage to the economy. It has also brought a sense of insecurity, fear, and fragmentation to our societies. According to the Institute for Strategic Dialogue (ISD), anti-migrant, and alt-right groups have exploited the outbreak to spread disinformation targeting migrants, refugees, and other vulnerable populations.

Alt-right extremists, like the boogaloo movement in the US are seeking to stoke the fear and disruption caused by the pandemic to push their agenda and recruit more members. To get their message across, these groups exploit loopholes in Facebook anti-violence policies – using satire, codewords, and other tactics that mask their motives.

COVID-19 has exposed inequalities and decline in mental health

According to a Eurofound, the European Foundation for the Improvement of Living and Working Conditions, publication of November 2020, significant inequalities between specific groups across the EU have emerged due to the pandemic. The generational divide in the labour market that resulted from the 2008-2009 global financial crisis is still present a decade later. Long-term youth unemployment is out of control, and the path to stable employment, security and homeownership has become more complex. The resilience of Europe's youth in dealing with a new crisis was already diminished before the COVID-19 crisis. Young people had a disproportionately high risk of depression, loneliness and anxiety during the pandemic than the rest of the population.

The worst-case scenario for the future is new epidemics of diseases just as contagious as COVID19, but even more deadly – or diseases for which we will not be able to produce vaccines. It seems that we are entering what Anthony Fauci, the director of the US National Institute of Allergy and Infectious Diseases, has called the "pandemic era", with an increasingly frequent transmission of diseases from wild and domestic animals.

Humanity lives in disharmony with nature. Phenomena such as overpopulation, urbanisation, global food supply chains, and increased global mobility favour the emergence and spread of new viruses. This is the reason there is a huge need for international cooperation, because something that happens 5,000 kilometres away can very quickly become a global problem.

Chapter 4

The Looting of Democracy

Our government does not copy our neighbours, but is an example to them. It is true that we are called a democracy, for the administration is in the hands of the many and not of the few.

— Thucydides: Pericles' Funeral Oration

Never since WWII has the planet experienced such an unstable environment. The effects of globalisation and global warming have changed the social, economic, and political situation. Terrorism, immigration, general insecurity, and the rise of populism and illiberal democracies have developed a mass fear that is destabilising the complex construction of the European Union, the US, and the West in general. Fear has taken over large parts of the population in many countries around the world.

It is by manipulating this anxiety that populists such us Nigel Farage, Marine Le Pen, Geert Wilders, or Matteo Salvini are trying to destroy everything Europe has ever built since the Treaty of Rome signed on 25 March 1957. The Treaty of Rome established the European Economic Community (EEC) which is seen as a major stepping stone in the creation of the EU. It established a common market giving its members the freedom to move goods, services, capital, and people and also a customs union among the founding states.

Outside European borders, a loose alliance of autocrats has been born with Putin of Russia, Erdogan of Turkey, and the Chinese leadership – all wanting to undermine the European project, NATO, and the West.

The chronic nervous breakdown of Donald Trump on Twitter

The same situation exists on the other side of the Atlantic. The last four years have been devastating for EU–US relations. Donald Trump does not see allies as important to the US-European security relationship and does not believe in the West or any kind of alliance. His persistent attacks on the European Union and NATO, and his constant degradation of allies in favour of authoritarian leaders such as Russian president Putin and Turkish president Erdogan who oppose the alliance, has meant that relations with Washington have never been so bad since 1945.

From the start, the most controversial US president has constantly lied, expressed admiration for dictators, denigrated, and threatened to jail his political opponents; belittled judges and other public officials; denigrated foreigners, demonised journalists, and provoked racial division. Trump also mixed his personal financial interests with government business, placed his children and son-in-law in positions of power, and frequently talked as if the government were his personal property. His presidency finally collapsed in shame after his baseless claims of electoral fraud and the Capitol insurrection failed.

"Mr. President, it's time to end this dark charade," the *New York Post* editorial board wrote in its edition of 28 December 2020. The tabloid, which endorsed Trump for president, asked Trump to "Give it up," adding "for your sake and the nation's". Before the election, a columnist for the newspaper, owned by Rupert Murdoch called Trump an "invincible hero".

During the past four years Trump governed via Twitter. "Without Twitter, there would be no Donald Trump presidency," said CNN senior political analyst Kirsten Powers, "and I think he knows that." Trump used Twitter to announce new policies, fire government officials, and attack his political opponents. As Nicholas Carr writes in *Politico* of 2 January 2018 Why Trump Tweets (And Why We Listen):

> "Trump's tweeting is best understood as an expression of a salesman's desire to shape reality to his own benefit. It is as inevitable as the gold leaf in his Trump Tower penthouse. More disturbing is the effect his tweeting continues to have on the rest of us. Rather than tune the messages out or dismiss them as distractions, the press, and the public seem more in their thrall than ever."

But why do people vote for right-wing populists like Donald Trump in the US, Nigel Farage in the UK, Viktor Orban in Hungary, or Bolsonaro in Brazil? And why does the rise of populism come at a time when most people say they are happy? Why do we have parties like Vlaams Belang – a far-right, anti-immigrant, anti-Islam party in Flanders (Belgium), which is one of the most prosperous regions in the world – that win 18.5% of the votes becoming the second largest party in Belgium at the 2019 federal elections?

It Can't Happen Here was the title of a 1930s novel about the United States. Fascism never came to America – nor is it likely to – but it was quite close with a second election of Donald Trump. As Edward Luce describes in his article of 4 June 2020 in the *Financial Times*:

> "Mr. Trump wants Americans to believe that the White House is threatened by domestic terrorists, arsonists, thugs, looters and killers – words he has used frequently in the past few days. US stability is under threat, he claims. The president's life, and those of decent law-abiding Americans, are threatened by the extremists on the streets. That is the gist of Mr. Trump's message. But it requires a visual backdrop. Hence the hyped-up situation in Washington."

Scholars of electoral behaviour regularly link political dissatisfaction to two types of behaviour: voting for populist parties and unstable voting behaviour. However, Remko Voogd and Ruth Dassonneville in their report published in Cambridge University Press, on 17 September 2018, argue that this is not necessarily the case –particularly in the context of increasingly strong and viable populist parties. They made use of data from the Comparative Study of Electoral Systems project to show that voters for populist parties are neither more nor less volatile than voters for mainstream parties. Political dissatisfaction among voters for populist parties even increases the likelihood of stable voting for populist parties.

This means that populism is best understood as a symptom of growing dissatisfaction with (liberal) democracies, which emerges when citizens believe that political institutions are unwilling or unable to respond to their needs and demands. In democracies, unlike in dictatorships, dissatisfied citizens can express their dissatisfaction by voting to change their leaders and governments.

A new Ground Zero

On Wednesday 6 January 2021, the entire planet was astonished as armed supporters of US President Donald Trump stormed the Capitol in Washington to stop lawmakers from confirming President-elect Joe Biden's electoral win –usually a ceremonial event.

The violent mob loyal to Donald Trump was earlier urged by the president – during a rally – to go to the Capitol. Had this happened in Chile, Thailand, or Haiti, it would be called an attempted coup. Following a particularly horrific year of anti-Black police brutality, the scenes were staggering as the police did little to discourage the violent action.

A few days earlier, the *Washington Post* released Trump's recorded call with Georgia secretary of state, Brad Raffensperger, where the former pressured the latter to "find [him] 11,780 votes" in order to overturn the election results in Georgia.

President Trump's refusal to concede to his successful challenger is "giving great comfort" to "authoritarian regimes" around the world, said Joe Biden's biographer on CNN. Trump's actions are a blow to the integrity of US democracy and democracy in general. It will have geopolitical implications on liberal democracies worldwide, especially in Europe, with the rise of alt-right movements and similar despots in Hungary and Poland.

Many questions arise. How can the US ask authoritarian countries to respect human rights when they are not even in a position to defend their prominent institutions properly? Will the US be able to tell the world that they are the paragon of democracy ever again? Democracy is not just about institutions. It is about political culture, too. All democratic countries need to constantly defend it. The reputation damage is gigantic, not only for the US but for the entire West!

Today's despotic societies are not fully formed dictatorships. They manufacture enemies and crises and extend political instability, keeping citizens in a situation of stress and trauma until they are exhausted and lose interest – while ensuring that autocrats can act with impunity.

The siege of the iconic Congress building is the result of the irresponsible, extreme, and violent far-right populism of the American president. It is the result of lies, state disinformation, and strategic propaganda reproduced by certain media and social media platforms. His party, which let things get so far, also shares the blame. Today, the "big democracy" looks like a Third World democracy.

In Europe, most leaders expressed shock, and dismay while seeing the chaos in Washington. "What happened today in Washington, D.C., is not America," French President Emmanuel Macron said in a video message on Twitter two days after the storming of Capitol Hill. "We believe in the strength of our democracies. We believe in the strength of American democracy."

Belgian Prime Minister Alexander De Croo condemned the violent riots at the Capitol building and expressed his support for Joe Biden. "Shock and disbelief at ongoing events at the US Capitol, symbol of American democracy. We trust the strong institutions of the United States will overcome this challenging moment. Full support to President-elect Joe Biden," he tweeted.

Heiko Maas, the German foreign minister, urged Trump supporters to "stop trampling" on democratic values. "The enemies of democracy will be pleased to see these incredible images from Washington, D.C.," he added.

European Union officials indicated their support for Biden as well:

"I believe in the strength of US institutions and democracy. A peaceful transition of power is at the core. Joe Biden won the election," Ursula von der Leyen, President of the European Commission, wrote on Twitter.

EU Council President Charles Michel described the US Congress as "a temple of democracy" and said to Biden, "We trust the US to ensure a peaceful transfer of power".

However, the most horrifying thing about the Washington attacks is not how easily Trump's far-right supporters invaded the Capitol despite openly stating that they wanted to prevent Biden from taking power and to eliminate those who "stole" the election – an election that the serving president had lost with a difference of seven million votes. Citizens have the right to know the truth and why security officials were so unprepared for the breach of the building, supposedly one of the most secure in the nation, despite serious warnings of potential violence. Also, the role of Republican lawmakers closely allied with Donald Trump in planning the "Stop the Steal" rally that spiralled into a brutal onslaught should be explored deeply. The most important question that we have to ask ourselves is how can the US prevent a similar scenario from happening again?

The "indignation" expressed by the bewitched mob doped by Trump's rhetoric in the corridors of the Capitol is the birth of American fascism, which has been in the making for many years now. Like all fascist movements, it presupposes a reference to a leader – in this case Trump – and the most chilling thing is that it will not disappear just because he has left Washington. We are watching something that has deeper roots than Trump himself.

Even more terrifying is the passivity of social media platforms during the four years of his presidency. They only waited until the attack on US institutions' to take measures against the spread of extreme hate speech and racism via their channels. In the aftermath of the Washington events, key opinion leaders around the world condemned Facebook, Twitter, and Google's YouTube for failing to stop the flood of extremist and dangerous content from Donald Trump and his supporters which fuelled the violence at Capitol Hill. Five people died during the siege, including a police officer.

Finally, Twitter, Facebook, and Instagram locked Donald Trump's accounts temporarily after posts with policy "violations" and widespread condemnation. Twitter locked the account for 12 hours and Facebook for 24 hours. Following this, Facebook and Instagram banned Trump's account from posting for at least the remainder of his term in office and perhaps "indefinitely" said Zuckerberg on a blog post.

On Friday 8 January, Twitter also suspended President Trump from its platform. "After close review of recent Tweets from the @realDonaldTrump account and the context around them we have permanently suspended the account due to the risk of further incitement of violence," Twitter said.

YouTube said on 12 January that it was suspending Trump's channel for at least one week for violating the company's policies. A recent video on Trump's channel had incited violence, YouTube told CNN Business. That video has now been removed. YouTube declined to share details of the video that earned Trump the strike, but said that after the one-week timeout, it would reconsider its decision.

In doing so, social media platforms recognised their responsibility in helping to prevent the spread of illegal and violent viral content. The Trump Twitter ban and Facebook's belated clampdown finally settles it: social media platforms should be seen as publishers, with all the responsibilities that go with that privilege. They can no longer hide their duty towards society by arguing that they only provide hosting services. The Capitol Hill siege exposes the fragility of our democracies and the threat tech companies can pose to their survival. There is an urgent need for regulation, not only in Europe but also in the US and the rest of the world. And, as Thierry Breton, the European Commissioner for the internal market writes in *Politico* (10 January 2021), "Just as 9/11 marked a paradigm shift for global security, 20 years later, we are witnessing a before-and-after in the role of digital platforms in our democracy".

As was the case in Germany and Italy in the 1930s, elites are responsible for the evolution we experience. American elites accepted to be represented by a racist. Trump would not have risen to power, nor would he have survived without the consent of powerful media owners, criminal strategists, and big financial interests. He survived thanks to corporate tax cuts, the support of a party which is in free fall and, the revocation of popular health, labour, and environmental policies.

However, the US is not alone. From Bolsonaro in Brazil to Erdogan in Turkey, Vladimir, and the Ayatollahs of Persia, for 20 years our liberal democracies have been under siege. A mixture of critical, extreme conservative, anti-systemic, and far-right movements has emerged, challenging the basic principles of liberal democracies.

To date, the West has failed in to stop this despicable transformation of our liberal world – which was formed between 1945 and 1991 – to illiberal societies. Brexit and Trump are children of the same mother. The creation of an international fascist movement that Trump tried to design with Steve Bannon, has failed for now, but the pirates are still out there awaiting the next opportunity to plunder democracy.

Liberal democracies in Europe, America, and the rest of the world should take measures to tackle this global threat and act fast. They should start by issuing strong legislation for the use and content on large social media platforms like Facebook, Twitter, YouTube, Instagram, etc. They should begin by making policies beneficial for all citizens and saving our planet from climate change and providing affordable health care and education for all.

Also, the attempted coup at the Capitol is a wake-up call for the big brands regarding the funding of online disinformation. Along with other forms of manipulative, anti-democratic communication, disinformation has emerged as a problem for Internet policy. Ad-funded disinformation by companies is possible as they don't know where their digital ads on Facebook, YouTube, or other sites will be run. One solution could be to cut down on the number of sites on which they advertise which might make vigilance more likely. Companies should be aware that they are responsible for where their logo shows up and what their ad budgets fund.

This is not about freedom of speech, political marketing, or entertainment. When people are sent out to belittle, attack, or kill others; when we are told that there are those who will steal our jobs, thus encouraging hate, this has nothing to do with free speech, it is called a crime. It is paramount for societies across the planetto respect the rule of law and political equality. This is about the survival of our civic freedoms, our values, and our democracies. We must create order in the chaos outside before it enters our house.

One of the greatest changes in US policy is that on the first day of his presidency, Joe Biden fulfilled his promise to rejoin the Paris Agreement and set a course for the United States to tackle the climate crisis at home and abroad, reaching net zero emissions economy-wide by no later than 2050. In his inauguration speech, Biden said America needed to respond to a "climate in crisis". The change in direction from the Trump era was profound and immediate.

Chapter 5

We Have a Dream

Europe, which for a long time triggered a yawn, today sparks a kitchen-table screaming match. Europe is the theatre of powerful, emotional, clashing forces that will shape our future.

— Bono

Is it really sixteen years ago that the European Union experienced its largest-ever round of enlargement? I have a fairly vivid recollection of 2004, a turning point in the history of the EU. On Saturday 1 May of that year capitals across Europe started celebrating the most considerable expansion in the history of the EU. I was then Press Officer at the EU Permanent Representation of Cyprus in Brussels.

A few weeks before, the permanent representative, Ambassador Theophilou, asked me to accompany Markos Kyprianou, the first appointed commissioner by Nicosia, to Romano Prodi's office, the President of the European Commission. It was spring and optimism for the continent's future was everywhere.

> "The 1st of May 2004 is a historic day for Europe. We welcome into the EU family ten new member countries and millions of new EU citizens. Five decades after our great project of European integration began, the divisions of the Cold War are gone – once and for all," said Prodi.

A huge variety of events, large and small, ranging from concerts and exhibitions to culinary fairs and debates were organised across Europe. In Brussels, the EU institutions organised an open door day, allowing visitors into the buildings and the meeting rooms of the Parliament, the Council, and the Commission. There were also festivities at the Grande Place and the Cinquantenaire Parc. I had to go from celebration to celebration as the Cyprus diplomatic missions in Brussels were represented at different events.

I will never forget the joy and satisfaction of that day. After seven years of extremely difficult and complex accession negotiations, Cyprus, a small, divided country, became a member of the EU. At the Cyprus diplomatic missions in Brussels, we had to fight without interruption on two fronts: the accession negotiations with the EU and the Cyprus problem, an outcome of the 1974 Turkish invasion and illegal occupation of 36% of its territory.

Saturday 1 May 2004 was set to reach a climax with the launch of hot air balloons in the colours of the EU countries. They were to be inflated, launched, and later return for a select night show. However, the wind was blowing in the wrong direction and they had to stay on the ground. This led some spectators to wonder aloud whether that was a good sign for the future of an enlarged EU.

Three years earlier, in November 2001, Prodi described his optimism about the expansion imperative. Speaking to the European Parliament in the presence of the EU Enlargement Commissioner, Gunter Verheugen, Prodi said enlargement would boost Europe's standing in a world that was "profoundly changed" by the 11 September terrorist attacks in New York. "With enlargement, we will be concluding a chapter of Europe's history and laying down the foundations for the future," he said.

Nowadays, attitudes towards further enlargement are contrary, both among EU citizens and member state governments. The 2004 enlargement that was so strongly associated with ending the division of Europe appears now to have a gloomy outlook for further integration and unification. The euro crisis divided Europe between the North and the South, and the refugee crisis is even worse for Europe. In addition to the North-South divide, an East versus West confrontation has arisen. Most European capitals were heartily disappointed when countries in Eastern Europe blankly refused to participate in a European solution to the refugee crisis. The European project is in the middle of its most severe crisis since the Treaty of Rome was signed by the six founding members in 1957.

On 23 June 2016, to the astonishment of the entire world, the UK decided in a referendum to leave the Union. British Prime Minister David Cameron had taken a gamble and lost. The world stock markets and the British pound crashed when the results of the referendum were published and the EU lost its second biggest economy. Cameron resigned and Scotland demanded independence. According to Martin Wolf of the

Financial Times, this was probably the most disastrous single event in British history since the Second World War.

After four and a half years of negotiations, the EU and the UK announced on Thursday 24 December 2020, Christmas Eve, that they had managed to agree on the terms of their future cooperation and a free trade agreement. The Brexit withdrawal deal contains new rules for how the EU and UK will live, work, and trade together.

However, Brexit was not only the result of the myths and the misinformation of Nigel Farage, Boris Johnson, Michael Gove, the British anti-European yellow press, or the 2004 enlargement. Since its very beginning, the European project has been challenged by all kinds of nationalism and populism. During the last seven years, the EU has failed to cope with significant challenges such as the euro crisis and the refugee issue.

Since the financial crisis exposed the structural shortcomings of the eurozone, Brussels' economic weakness has been one of the key arguments against EU membership in Great Britain, just as the Union's economic strength was a key argument for accession in the 1975 referendum. The austerity-driven economy, the premature enlargement with East and Central Europe countries and the arrivals of tens of thousands of refugees from the Middle East and North Africa, have all proved to be fatal for European cohesion and further integration.

It would appear that the EU and its member states are not up to the many challenges emerging simultaneously, whether it concerns unemployment, taxation, terrorism, immigration, homegrown political extremism, the unity of the eurozone, economic growth, or even Europe's military cooperation.

A significant inadequacy of the European Union is the way it communicates. Brussels faces considerable difficulties due to a lack of political participation by its citizens and the lack of involvement of its citizens has become a serious concern. Little interest in politics, poor knowledge of political processes, low levels of trust in politicians, and growing cynicism of democratic institutions are often seen as indicators of the weakened sense of citizenship and political engagement present in our society.

The European Union is not engaging; rather, it is perceived as boring and irrelevant. European citizens do not understand what is happening in Brussels and the Union fails to deliver when it comes to communication at the national, regional, European, and global levels.

The founders of the European project were dreamers. They dreamed of a united Europe: a continent of peace, solidarity, and shared prosperity. A Europe without borders and divisions that celebrates the continent's incredible diversity. A Europe evolving towards an ever closer union, inspired by the notion that Europe will always be stronger together.

Europe has been undergoing a process of slow unification for almost seven decades now and is better off for it. There is less conflict between European countries than at any time in history, and their collective power makes Europe strong – even now in the era of coronavirus.

The European Union has brought freedom, justice, and sustainable democracy, and helps protect our basic political, social, and economic rights. Citizens living in the EU have the same rights in all other member states as they do in their country of origin. Europeans can travel, study, reside, and work in the other member states. They can even vote in certain elections in other EU countries.

Although disappointed by the way the EU treated Greece's debt crisis, the lack of leadership and European politicians' inability to work together, I believe that a united Europe constitutes the only sustainable and viable future for the continent. Nevertheless, the European Union must change and adapt itself to contemporary challenges. There is a democratic deficit in Europe and this is related to the lack of a common European public sphere and sustainable communication. There is not enough common space for the citizens of the various nations to become involved in EU politics.

Is the EU falling Apart?

Let's face it. The primary disruptive element of the European Union is its structure. Originally built to become a real federation with its own institutions, it was rerouted by Paris when the French Parliament rejected the creation of a European Defence Community (EDC) in August 1954. At present, the European Union is a free association of sovereign states designed to cooperate to achieve their shared aims. Other than the goal of "ever closer union" in the Solemn Declaration of the EU (1983), the Union has no specific policy to create either a federation or a confederation.

In 2015, the world witnessed the short career of Yanis Varoufakis as Finance Minister of Greece. I met the rock-star economist turned politician during a debate about the euro crisis at the hotel Le Chatelain in Brussels in June 2015. To be honest, I had never heard of him before he was appointed as minister and was keen to hear more about his ideas.

Varoufakis reminded me of Lucky Luke – the cartoon character created by the Belgian cartoonist Morris – although he looked more like Rantanplan. While always described as a cowboy, Lucky Luke generally acts like a person who advocates rights. To a broad public in Greece and other European countries too Varoufakis appeared to be a Lucky Luke arriving on his Yamaha motorbike to rescue them from austerity.

In his book, *And the Weak Suffer What They Must?* The former economic adviser of Greek PM George Papandreou presents a detailed historical analysis of the origins of Europe's financial crisis. He describes the eurozone as a construction that does not lead to shared prosperity, as was intended, but "as a pyramid scheme of debt with countries such as Greece, Ireland, Portugal and Spain at its bottom". The book concludes that Europe "is too important to be left to its clueless rulers", and that the eurozone must be fully recalibrated if Europe is to avoid a repetition of the 1930s, with financial chaos, conflict, and the rise of fascism.

Varoufakis may be an excellent economist; nevertheless, as a politician, he failed to convince that his propositions might have been interesting. His extravagant comments in referring to the EU's treatment of Greece as "fiscal waterboarding" or his comparison of the eurozone to the Titanic made him look untrustworthy and arrogant at that time. He did not quite succeed in adopting a constructive diplomatic language or to demonstrate credibility based on evidence-based arguments and content.

Still, the former Greek finance minister is not against the European Union. In 2016, he launched a new pan-European grassroots political movement, the Democracy in Europe Movement 2025 (DiEM25), aiming to democratise Europe. According to its manifesto, DiEM25 wants to "bring about a fully democratic, functional Europe by 2025, as an alternative to a common bureaucracy and a common currency which divides European peoples that were beginning to unite despite our different languages and cultures".

Intellectually Dr Varoufakis is for some more attractive than far-right anti-EU populists like Nigel Farage, Geert Wilders, Marine Le Pen, or Viktor Orban. However, his brief appearance in the European political arena has more to do with the failure of the EU to give answers to the citizen's concerns, than with his political ideology.

Politicians in Europe and other parts of the world have adopted extreme views to gain the support of an anxious and angry electorate. Traditional centre parties are collapsing and in countries like Hungary, Poland, and Brazil, right-wing parties have taken over the reins of government. In Hungary, the populist government of Viktor Orban is a major opponent of immigration. As *The Economist* writes, "he cast Christian Europe as battling Muslim hordes for survival, stirring memories of ancient battles against Ottoman invaders and shattering political taboos".

The Hungarian Prime Minister organised a referendum in October 2016 on whether to accept the mandatory quotas for refugees passed by the EU last year. Under EU agreements, the decision to institute relocation quotas is binding. However, Orban said that doing so without consulting his nation's citizens was an abuse of power. In the end, Viktor Orban failed to convince a majority of the population to vote on closing the door to refugees. The referendum was invalid as almost 60% of the voters stayed at home.

Hungary, which built a fence on its southern border to keep out refugees, has repeatedly accused the EU of weakness to face the crisis, calling for hard policies such as fortified borders and severe immigration procedures. Around a month before the referendum the country was full of anti-migrant messages on billboards and on state television as the government was seeking widespread support for its opposition to the migrant relocation quotas between EU member states. Leaflets about the referendum were delivered by mail to all voters.

Budapest's hate campaign has been developed in real 1930's propaganda style with taglines like: "Did you know that since the start of the immigration crisis, more than 300 people in Europe died in terror attacks?" or "Did you know that just from Libya, nearly a million immigrants want to come to Europe?" Lookingat the outcome of the referendum, though, we can say with confidence that it failed.

In the first round of the French regional elections on 6 December 2015, the far-right anti-EU Front National (FN), narrowly gained the largest share of the national vote. The FN's leader, Marine Le Pen, and her niece each polled over 40%.

In Spain, the anti-establishment Podemos party, founded in March 2014, has become one of the three largest political parties in the country. In Greece, Prime Minister Alexis Tsipras of the left-wing Syriza party has been leading a strange coalition with the right-wing populist Independent Greeks (ANEL) between 2015 and 2019.

The blind belief in austerity measures and the inability of the Union to manage major crises with a united and coherent voice is leading to the further disintegration of the European project. For example, following a report by the Bank of Greece (July 2016) since the crisis struck Greece in 2009, more than 427,000 young, educated professionals – a group with more than 50% unemployment – have left the country.

In Greece, thousands of enterprises have closed down. In July 2016, Kyriakos Mamidakis, chairman of Jetoil, one of the most prominent and iconic entrepreneurs of the country, committed suicide. A few days earlier, Jetoil requested court protection from creditors as it was unable to make payments on its debt. The company had a network of 600 gas stations in Greece, a fleet of 33 tanker trucks and seven ships for supplying islands and vessels, and owned the largest single storage site in the Balkans.

In May 2015, I interviewed the president of the Academy of Athens, which is the nation's most prestigious research organisation, Dimitri Nanopoulos. He said that bureaucracy and cronyism dominate Greece and the EU. Nanopoulos compared the past seven years of economic turmoil to the Greek civil war in the late 1940s and the period of military rule between 1967 and 1974.

In July 2016, concerns about the bad state of Italian banks added to Brexit concerns across global financial markets. The figures suggest an astonishing 17% of bank loans in Italy are bad, equal to €360 billion of bad credit. This is much more compared with the debt held during the 2008 financial crisis. That is, for example, nearly ten times the level in the USA, which was only 5% even at the most dangerous moment of the 2008–09 financial crisis.

I am not quite sure which year was the worst for Europe. Was it 2015, 2016, or 2020? The euro crisis, the refugee problem, the outcome of the British referendum to reject EU membership, or the COVID-19 crisis? While the economic consequences of Brexit are not to be dismissed, it is the imminent failure of the European project that should cause a bigger sense of concern. The two greatest achievements of the EU since the establishment of the single market, the euro and the Schengen Area, are both under threat. If the euro and border-free travel implode, it would be much more painful than the UK vote.

However, there is hope that the populist tide is turning. After the results of the 2019 Slovakian presidential race were released on 30 March 2019, Zuzana Caputova, then president-elect, and a pro-European liberal, told a crowd of supporters: "I am happy not just for the result but mainly that it is possible not to succumb to populism". The anti-corruption activist and leader of the Progressive Slovakia (PS) party was sworn in on 15 June 2019 as the country's first female president.

Amidst the populist upsurge across European democracies, Caputova's election offers hope that a populist takeover is not inevitable and that democratic backsliding can be reversed. The most important lesson from her victory is that civil resistance works. Her election should be seen as the achievement of a national resistance against democratic erosion. It was the mass street protests following the murder of journalist Jan Kuciak, who was investigating high-level corruption inside the ruling Smer party, that propelled Caputova to power.

In September 2016, I attended a debate on the consequences of Brexit in Brussels with Guy Verhofstadt, the President of the Alliance of Liberals and Democrats for Europe (now Renew Europe) at the European Parliament, and Sandro Gozi, Italian Under-Secretary for European Affairs. Guy Verhofstadt reiterated previous declarations that we cannot defend this kind of Europe anymore.

> "The EU needs to reform and a new project should be presented to the people. European citizens are not against Europe. They are against the type of Europe we have now. People want a Union capable of handling the big crises we are facing today like the euro

crisis and the refugee's crisis. A reform of the European Union is needed and we need it now," he said.

It seems evident to me that this Union cannot go any further. A free association of states such as it is now does not work. To face global challenges and be a world player, Europe needs a better structure and sustainable policy. There is a need for a new Europe that is in a position to cope with the most significant issues we face today: globalisation, unemployment, health issues like COVID-19, migration, security, global warming, and terrorism. We need a genuine European government and a parliament directly elected by the people to secure the economy and protect the borders of the continent.

The Art of Perception

The difference between mere management and leadership is communication.

— Winston Churchill

Soon everyone on planet Earth will be connected. With five billion more people set to join the digital world, the boom in online connectivity is bringing changes in professions, quality of life, health, productivity, and many other areas. The future will be shaped by how states, citizens, corporations, and institutions handle their new responsibilities.

Communication itself has also undergone many changes. Communicators have had to adapt to new media and learn to use digital communication and the Internet. Online public communication has become an essential part of any successful government policy. The reality of modern communications is that citizens expect to have digital experiences which work anywhere and anytime, and are personalised to their needs.

Institutions within the EU are aware of the growing influence of digital and social media on citizens and organisations. They use social media, websites, and video to reach out and connect with citizens and stakeholders, in addition to the communication which takes place via the traditional channels such as press releases, broadcast media, and EU publications.

The lack of a shared vision seems to be more harmful to the European project than is commonly acknowledged. The EU does not rely – as a real state does – on a common language, a pure common history, or real ethnic bonds to ensure its legitimacy and continuity. It is a self-willed community, a cultural union, a project of shared values and objectives.

During the preparation of my book *Rebranding Europe* (2017), I spoke to prominent figures in EU communications and discovered that although some initiatives have been set up during the last years, there is room for improvement in Europe's communications.

George Kasimatis, head of *EuroparlTV* (http://www.europarltv.europa.eu/en/home.aspx), the web TV of the European Parliament, finds that it has taken some time for EU institutions to realise the importance of communicating with its citizens.

"Delaying the process of communicating with the people led us to a situation that citizens were not part of the European project," he said. "If you want people to support the European project, you have to make them part of this project. We have realised this during the European elections of 2009 and 2014. The participation decreased all over Europe to less than 50% of the citizens. The challenge for the EU is to continue to have better and more enhanced communication, and helping citizens understand that Europe concerns all of us and that we all should be part of it," he added.

The first websites of the three main EU institutions, the European Parliament, The European Commission, and the Council of the EU, were launched in 2006, together with the Europa website (https://europa.eu/). The European Parliament (https://twitter.com/Europarl_EN) joined Twitter in 2009, followed by the Commission (https://twitter.com/EU_Commission) and the Council in 2010. It was also the European Parliament that first started with an account on Facebook in 2009 followed by the European Commission in 2011 and the Council in 2012. European Commission Vice President for the Digital Market, Andrus Ansip (https://twitter.com/Ansip_EU) launched his very first EU Twitter chat in 2014.

Online media covering EU affairs like *Euractiv* (www.euractiv.com) and *EUobserver* (https://euobserver.com) appeared in the first half of the 2000s. *European Voice*, changed to *Politico* (http://www.politico.eu) in 2014, is a weekly founded in 1995 and reports on the EU in printed and digital versions. *New Europe*, (www.neweurope.eu) founded in 1993, is a weekly reporting on European affairs and has a digital and a paper version. An interesting site of the European Commission concerning social media – which unfortunately was archived in November 2014 – worth visiting is Waltzing Matilda, a blog created by teams working in web and social media for the European Commission to share new ideas, challenges, and progress in being digital as an institution (https://ec.europa.eu/archives/commission_2010-2014/blogs/waltzing_matilda/).

Digital technology has tremendous potential and impact on EU communication. As people become more connected and more demanding, EU institutions are responsible for keeping pace with the developments and keeping with digital transformation. In 2013 the European Commission (EC) created a significant cross-Commission programme of digital transformation to redesign and redefined its online communication. In its vision for digital transformation (http://blogs.ec.europa.eu/eu-digital) the European Commission believes that digital communication channels can bring the EU closer to the people: "A strong digital presence will help us be more relevant, coherent, and transparent while giving the institution a more human face."

The massive EU enlargement of 2004 with countries of a different political and socioeconomic culture, European disputes on the euro, the refugee crisis, austerity, and the departure of Great Britain from the Union, have all created a major social and political cacophony in Europe. Also, we have to admit that the EU is a complex organisation that is not easily explained.

The European Union is a complex and unique construction with many more institutions, processes, and policy actors than other international organisations. Other global and regional organisations like the UN and the Council of Europe do not have such a broad range of responsibilities as the EU. They are essentially intergovernmental in character while the Union has more supranational aspects. That does not make the EU a state, but a highly developed regional organisation and political system.

Too many voices

There is no lack of online news and information on the EU and its policies. On the contrary, the communication problem lies in the availability of the vast amount and wide range of insufficiently clear or understandable information without clear priorities. This results in a situation where information overload loses its informative objective, leading to misinformation.

The European Commission, the European Parliament, the Council of the EU, the Court of Justice, the European Economic and Social Committee, the Committee of the Regions, etc. have their websites, social media profiles, and other digital channels. However, they are still facing difficulties in attracting the attention of the citizens.

The EU has more than 40 agencies divided into four groups (decentralised, executive, and Euratom agencies, and those under common security and defence policy); and all are distinct bodies from the EU institutions. That means that they are separate legal entities set up to perform specific tasks under EU law. These agencies play a key role in implementing EU policies and contributing to the EU's overall visibility and image. For many agencies, external communication is a core task. They can disseminate information and research-based evidence on specific issues, trends, and challenges which relate to EU policy and its implementation, only through communication activities to inform policymakers and the public.

In addition, the EU member states have different attitudes of public opinion, depending on their historical, socioeconomic, political, or media context. Depending on these factors, citizens have different feelings concerning their place within the EU or delegating power to it. This leads to different expectations and when these are not met, the perception of the EU changes.

The huge gap of communication between the European Union and its citizens is not new. It has been a subject of discussion since the Maastricht Treaty of 1992. After the decrease in participation in the European elections in 2004 and the rejection of the referendums on the European Constitution in France and the Netherlands in 2005, the EU, and more specifically, the EC, decided to reformulate its communication policy. In this regard, the Commission proposed a new approach aimed at communication becoming a policy on its own. The idea was to move from an institution-centred monologue to a citizen-centred dialogue; a communication in the service of citizens based on reinforced dialogue between the people and the policymakers. The 2004–09 European Commission was the first and only Commission to make communication a strategic objective. The Action Plan to Improve Communicating Europe included a specific list of measures to take in order to improve the way that the European Commission communicates with the citizens.

Plan D was launched in October 2005. It was a plan for dialogue, debate, and democracy that set out a process aimed at encouraging a broader debate on the future of the EU between the EU institutions and the people. Communicating Europe in Partnership was signed in December 2008. It was the first time that the three main EU institutions – Commission, Parliament, and Council – agreed to communicate Europe under a joint declaration. The four priorities selected were the European elections, energy and climate change, the 20th anniversary of democratic change in Central and Eastern Europe, and sustaining growth, jobs, and solidarity, with a particular link to the European Year of Creativity and Innovation.

Despite these improvements, EU communication policy is still not governed by specific provisions in the treaties but stems naturally from the EU's obligation to explain its functioning and policies, as well as European integration more generally, to the public. The need for effective communication has a legal basis in the Charter of Fundamental Rights of the EU, which guarantees the right of the people to be informed about European issues.

Jane Morrice, former Vice President of the European Economic and Social Committee (EESC) responsible for communications (2013–15) and former BBC correspondent, told me that the EU needs to communicate better and more:

> "We need a new plan for communicating Europe. We don't need another Plan D for European communication; we need an A to Z. It is essential! Europe has been very bad at communicating itself. It has been very bad blowing its own trumpet. If you take for

example America, this is a place that blows its trumpet every day, but Europe does not do it."

Accuracy, authenticity, and interest

The way in which communication is planned and resourced will determine the effectiveness and impact of the message. Too often, communication is seen purely as a support function aiming to disseminate messages at the end of a process. Successful communication can only happen therefore if communication and stakeholder relations are brought together early at the beginning of the process, that is, the actual drafting of EU policy or a project. This means setting the right institutional culture, supported by the right structures and resources.

It is paramount to align communication priorities and objectives at EU level and, foster a culture of collaboration among the different EU institutions, agencies, and other bodies. Communication departments should have a crucial role in assessing the policy and stakeholder relevance of a project or a policy and decide on key messages and target audiences as well as types of products and communication channels.

"Accuracy, Authenticity and Interest" was the slogan of Ivy Lee, one of the founding fathers of public relations, creator of the press release and pioneer in the field of crisis communications. Almost 100 years later, this slogan remains at the core of sustainable public relations. Though it takes many years to be built, a corporate or institutional reputation can be damaged quickly. This can happen to any organisation, including a supranational union like the EU.

Even though the EU has given almost 70 years of peace in Europe, the 2015 euro crisis paradoxically has been its most significant media breakthrough. People across the world started to follow EU-related news because of the consequences of the euro crisis. In recent years, the EU has spent a lot of time and money communicating with its citizens and explaining its policies and its *raison d'être*.

Nevertheless, the information and communication messages were full of jargon and the impact was poor. In her book *The Politics of Everyday Europe* (2015), Kathleen McNamara argues that the EU needs greater democratic representation, more citizen participation, and a higher quality of debate. "The EU needs more overt contestation and direct discussion of its policies, and debate over its leaders," she writes.

Jean-Claude van Damme and Jean-Claude Juncker: Same combat

Jane Morrice believes that the EU needs to communicate more and in a simpler way, and is in urgent need of more resources to do so.

"When I started working for the European Commission back in 1992, it was all about communicating with the citizens. Now, many decades later, we are still not properly communicating with the people. And I think that is because we are not speaking their language. We can start talking about things like jobs and money, but even that isn't stuff you talk about in the pub in the evening. And for some reason, the EU in Brussels does not know what people talk about in the pubs, whether it is in Galicia or Malta or somewhere in Eastern Europe. Brussels does not seem to connect with what ordinary people are talking about, nor speak their language," she said. "Start speaking the language of the street, start understanding the needs of ordinary people who do not know what Brussels is."

"I said to my hairdresser, in Northern Ireland, that I am working a lot in Brussels. I asked him what he knows about Brussels. He said the only thing he knows about it is Jean-Claude Van Damme. There is a perfect example. He did not pick Brussels,

Europe, or the European institutions, but a film star. We have to totally change the way we look at passing on information. Why do we not use Jean-Claude Van Damme for something? He is used for beer ads. Isn't he? There is a company who realises the value of him. Why can Europe not think that way? We are professional communicators who know how to get the messages across. That is what we need to do. To get a new way of approaching the European message," she added.

I am not quite sure if the hairdresser was confused because of the name of Jean-Claude Van Damme and the one of Jean-Claude Juncker. While the first is a Belgian actor known for his martial arts action films, the second was the European Commission president.

In June 2014, I found myself seated next to EU Commissioner Maria Damanaki, during a networking dinner at the Brussels hotel Le Chatelain. As a communications expert, I was asked if I had any suggestions for re-branding eurozone countries in financial trouble, in particular Greece. At the time, I was working on a Young & Rubicam project.

My answer was that the practice of public relations starts with policy, actions, and performance. PR, communication, and branding work properly when the product is good and the message is clear. It is necessary to make messages coherent, clear, concrete, and free from jargon and, connect them to particular human needs and expectations. Messages to send out should be carefully thought and tailored based on the target audience. However, if the policies are not right and not in the public interest, you have to change them. This is what politicians should recognise about the practice of communications.

Communicating Europe is all about democracy. Transparency is essential to democracy. People need to see how leaders are elected. Despite efforts to improve transparency, the process of selecting the president of the European Commission is still not transparent. The whole Brussels bubble is not very transparent, and only a few understand what is going on there – except those inside the two square km around the Schuman Roundabout. There is an urgent need for more transparency where EU affairs are concerned. Furthermore, EU governments and political leaders should stop the blame game when tough decisions need to be taken.

Good communication works when it is legitimated. "This Time is Different" (https://www.youtube.com/watch?v=UslDVJ2QSVM), was the slogan for one of the largest EU campaigns in regard to the May 2014 European elections. Unfortunately, it did not work. The campaign with its overall neutrality and sober and surreal image failed to adapt successfully to the social, political, and cultural diversity of the different member states.

However, differentiation is the holy grail of marketing. When a successful brand is launched, the first thing to rise is its level of differentiation. Despite the 2014 campaign, the votes for Eurosceptic parties increased and the abstention rate was historically high.

The rise of pan-European parties

Things changed in 2019. Turnout across the whole of the EU was 51%. This was higher than at any election in the last 20 years, although it remained lower than in the earliest elections to the European Parliament between 1979 and 1994. The two largest political groups in the European Parliament, the centre-right European People's Party (EPP) and the centre-left Socialists & Democrats (S&D) both suffered losses across the EU.

The liberal ALDE Group made gains thanks partly to the inclusion of French President Macron's *En Marche!* party and increased vote shares. Alt-right populist parties from the Europe of Nations and Freedom (ENF) Group did particularly well in Italy and France, where the League, and National Rally were the leading national parties.

Also, Europe is witnessing a transnationalisation of the parliamentary elections. The political centre has been weakening, and anti-establishment parties have been gaining ground across the continent. Pan-European policy debates have become more prominent and new pan-European parties have emerged, suggesting that Europe has the potential to outgrow its various nationalisms. For the first time, Europeans could vote for very different visions for the EU championed by real pan-European parties.

The leftist DiEM25/European Spring strives for fundamental democratic reform of the EU; Volt Europa has managed to mobilise particularly younger activists across the continent with a simple, pro-European and "post-ideological" message.

The EU is supposed to be a political union, which means that there should be a United political sphere or a European public sphere. Yet this is not the case. The European Parliament comprises groups, that are basically conglomerates of national political parties with different national interests that run campaigns at home, often on national issues, and then come to work together on policymaking in the European Parliament.

The restoration of public approval for the EU and boosting people's engagement are political and communication challenges that should become top priorities. Citizens should be brought closer to the EU and large-scale genuine pan-European parties might be the best solution.

Chapter 7

The Future of Europe

L'Europe se cherche. Elle sait qu'elle a en ses mains son propre avenir. Jamais elle n'a été si près du but. Qu'elle ne laisse pas passer l'heure de son destin, l'unique chance de son salut.

— Robert Schumann

Already from the start of the European Coal and Steel Community in the 1950s, many saw a future for further European integration. An ambitious idea of integration is Europe becoming a federation, the United States of Europe. The European Union has brought freedom, justice, and sustainable democracy, and helps protect our basic political, social, and economic rights. It has also supported the extraordinary transformation of former dictatorships in Europe, which are now members of the EU family.

South European countries previously with a democratic deficit and dictatorships like Spain, Greece, and Portugal are now examples of democracy. People with different political opinions in these countries are no longer in jail or exile. The European Union has also embraced former communist countries in Central and Eastern Europe. After decades living under communist regimes, they are under the secure umbrella of the Union.

The Union has achieved extraordinary results in the fields of education, environment, research, and innovation. However, in other fields like the creation of jobs, public diplomacy, and illegal immigration – one of the public's major concerns   it has failed to fulfil citizens' expectations and give answers with a united voice.

Despite the European Union ensuring more than 70 years of peace in Europe, the EU struggles to sell its story. Most Europeans see it as boring and often don't understand what is happening in Brussels. The EU and its member states have failed to communicate the added value of integration, cohesion, and cooperation: the advantages of common policies in the fields of finance, taxation, defence, trade, healthcare, and foreign affairs.

Europe is missing a sustainable strategy. To establish a strong relationship with the people, effective communication practices must be put in place.

A powerful connection with the citizens cannot be installed without a well thought out communication strategy and effective tools, practices, and analysis. Government policies rarely succeed when communication fails. Many factors contribute to inefficient communication: the lack of leadership, the absence of a shared vision and a common European public sphere, poor knowledge of EU affairs, a hostile media, EU red tape, unethical practices in politics, the "blame game" on European issues, multilingualism, and austerity. All these factors have contributed to the EU's incapability to communicate its policies and achievements in a transparent and clear way.

Today, audiences are central to the success of an organisation or a project. People no longer accept being "talked at". But EU communication is often based on one-way information, rather than genuine dialogue. To be successful, there is a need for change: the European message should be interesting to the media and understandable to citizens. The Parliament, the Commission, and the Council often express diverging and even contradictory views, resulting in a cacophony. "Europe can only work if we all work for unity and commonality, and forget the rivalry between competences and institutions. Only then will Europe be more than the sum of its parts," said Jean-Claude Juncker in his 2016 State of the Union speech.

Nevertheless, there are some successful methods for communicating Europe in a productive way such as, for example, the Citizens Dialogues. These public debates with European Commissioners and other EU decision-makers, such as members of the European Parliament and national, regional, and local politicians are very useful. The events take the form of a question and answer session. Citizens can ask EU politicians questions, make comments, and relate how EU policies affect them. They can also share their ideas on the future of Europe. Held in cities across the EU, the sessions are free to attend and many of these are broadcast live online.

A successful campaign that I also like is Invest EU, which tells the stories behind EU support: projects that got off the ground, new jobs, modern schools, and universities, efficient transport infrastructure, greener energy, and innovation throughout Europe.

The Conference on the Future of Europe

A tremendous chance to communicate the European project accurately is the upcoming Conference on the Future of Europe – originally an idea of French President Emmanuel Macron. While EU institutions were negotiating its mandate, composition, and the methodology of working, its launch on 9 May 2020 did not take place due to the coronavirus crisis and a lack of enthusiasm from some EU countries.

On 4 March 2021, EU leaders finally signed off on a plan to launch the Conference. The discussion forum will give citizens a chance to shape how the European Union will look in ten or twenty years from now. I hope the agreed structure will not kill the original idea of a bottom-up approach.

Overseeing the Conference will be a three-strong Joint Presidency composed of the presidents of the Commission and Parliament, as well as the EU's rotating Council presidency. An Executive Board will then make "decisions by consensus", assisted by a "Common Secretariat". The board will have nine members representing the Commission, Parliament, and Council, and "up to four observers". The three EU presidents will oversee the process while the Executive Board members will be in charge of making the Conference work. Additionally, a "Conference Plenary" will meet "at least every six months" to ensure that citizens' recommendations are debated.

I am not certain that extra bureaucracy with a "Joint Presidency", an "Executive Board", a "Conference Plenary", and a "Common Secretariat" will solve the EU's already confusing bureaucratic ills. Although I believe that the selection of Guy Verhofstadt as president was an excellent choice in the first place as he is a committed European and has long experience in EU affairs, however, now the whole project is more confusing. Nevertheless, Guy Verhofstadt will be one of the three presidents – representing the European Parliament and leading a group of seven MEPs, including two Eurosceptics.

Despite the warnings that expectations would not be met, as was the case with the European Constitution, and the additional bureaucracy, I still believe that the Conference is a unique opportunity towards a more democratic, sovereign, and federal Europe. It will offer the possibility of placing the future of the EU at the heart of the European debate and, if managed well, it could revitalise the European idea. The Conference is a wonderful project for recognising and respecting different national dimensions. It will be a process of discussion and citizen interaction, and should lead to the formulation of new ideas and capital reforms.

The member states of the EU have different public opinions depending on their historical, political, socioeconomic, and media contexts. The Conference on the Future will help us determine why a large number of Europeans do not endorse the Union. It will launch a discussion on what is the European identity and what our values are. We should use the process and the outcomes to communicate a message of unification in a coherent way – by considering the diversity of audiences and countries.

The Conference on the Future of Europe could be an excellent example of *Going Local*. Empowering citizens and engaging with them, supporting the development of a public European sphere, setting up a two-way dialogue, listening to the people, and being transparent. The outcomes of this democratic process should not be neglected but respected and analysed.

While the European Parliament was the first EU institution to publish a document on the Conference, in fact, President Macron came up with the original idea. For the moment, everybody wants to be involved, and so the discussion is currently focused on format rather than content.

Debate on the future of Europe is not new. Last time it was in 2017. The EC's White Paper on the Future of Europe was a sad confirmation of the absence of a future vision and leadership. Brussels cannot find a solution for the deadlock we have been in for many years. Nevertheless, most of the main actual problems such as the migrant crisis, Euroscepticism, co-operation on security issues, and lately the coronavirus pandemic require a coordinated European answer.

The Conference will focus on involving civil society in large debates about the future of Europe and provide sustainable solutions on how the Union can respond to peoples' needs. It should identify what the EU does well and what new measures need improvement to increase its capacity to act and to make it more democratic. The whole process should be based on a bottom-up approach. The six agoras foreseen will deliberate throughout the Conference process on a set of predefined policy areas, such as the digital transformation, social justice, climate crisis, the redrafting of EU electoral law, etc.

It should also provide more insights in fields concerning the transparency of the works of the EU Council; push forwards the system of pan-European lists for the next European elections and resurrect the system of *Spitzenkandidaten.*

The Conference should be a useful step in the direction of structuring a public European sphere. Such a sphere is hardly needed for the further unification of the continent. For the moment, Europe is not yet one nation and the EU is not yet a federal state. It is a kind of confederation. The absence of a real common European sphere is a huge obstacle for integration and cohesion. At the EU level, the identity component common in most European countries is very weak. If EU countries need an institutional setting to manage their interdependence while forgetting to build a common *demos*, infusing democracy into the system might be ineffective.

The absence of a European public opinion, related to the incompleteness of a European identity and the ever constant enlargement of the EU to new national public spheres, makes a common future and communication even more complicated. Communication implies the existence of a community. Despite improvements, the EU has often been unable to send clear and comprehensible messages to its citizens, focusing too much on who they are rather than what they do. All too often, they hide behind the complexities of policymaking or platitudes and fail to show why the EU matters and makes people's lives better.

Here are seven recommendations to help productively communicate Europe during and after the two years of the Conference:

(a) Make communication a strategic priority

A Brussels correspondent indicated in the survey described in my book *Rebranding Europe* (2017), the Leave Brexit campaign as the most successful one in the EU. During the first Barroso Commission, communication was an EU strategic priority and had a dedicated commissioner. Nowadays, that portfolio no longer exists. In the private sector, the Chief Communication Officer sits more and more at the C-level table when strategic or business decisions are made. The role of communication managers is to explain the implications of political, economic, societal, and technological changes to people's lives. Recently, over the last few years, we have seen examples of how it has worked in the public sector: in the US, Donald Trump–Steve Bannon, and in the UK, Boris Johnson–Dominic Cummings. The EU should make communication one of its top priorities. Strategic communication planning is a powerful management activity for identifying issues, setting priorities, defining strategies, and determining performance benchmarks as well as expectations.

(b) Communicate at both EU and national levels

Communicating in a true partnership is paramount. It needs to be based on common values, political will, transparency, and honesty. The key players should operate on an equal footing. An innovative and sustainable public–private partnership involving EU institutions, member states, civil society, the media, political parties, academia, and the private sector, would help. All parties would commit to presenting the EU as a useful brand, an entity that is seeking to collaborate with citizens and make a meaningful difference in their daily lives. The message should be adapted to the local identity of each country.

(c) Forget the fluff

Good communication is like good journalism: it creates transparency by making important things clear and relevant to stakeholders. Good communication helps create dialogue and is the basis of beneficial decision-making. It is necessary to make messages coherent, clear, concrete, and jargon-free, and to connect them to particular human needs and expectations. Speaking with one voice at all levels – EU, local and regional – is fundamental. If you want the attention of the audience the message needs to be clear.

(d) Talk about success

Over the last few years, we have heard different EU and national leaders expressing criticism about the European project. This sounds logical in times of crisis and this tendency is reinforced by the media which covers more the negative aspects of the crises. Nevertheless, there is an urgent need to also talk about good results. And there are plenty in the EU in the fields of education, research, innovation, etc. Messages of success will always be positive irrespective of the communication tools used to transmit them. Focus on what brings Europeans together. Focus on culture, education, humanitarian aid, and research.

(e) Support quality journalism and press independence, and challenge myths and populism

According to the March 2018 Eurobarometer on fake news and online disinformation, 85% of EU citizens perceive fake news as a problem in their country, 83% perceive it as a problem for democracy in general, and 73% are concerned about disinformation online during pre-election periods. Fundamental questions arise about social media platforms' approach to data protection and disclosure. There is an urgent need for a strategy for sustainable and independent media on the whole European continent. The EU and governments of the member states should support quality journalism on the one hand and challenge myths and populism on the other. In our European societies, in which citizens have not had many direct experiences with politics, mass media and increasingly social media are the most important channels for the creation of a public sphere and public opinion.

(f) Focus on what matters to the people

Traditional branding is based on the idea of what differentiates a company from the competition. A brand grows by promoting itself as different and isolating itself from others. Apple, for example, took that quite literally to great success with the *Think different* campaign. However, people are comfortable on the Internet with the idea that everything is interconnected. So what distinguishes brands becomes less important than what brings things and people together. It does not really matter if your iPhone can talk to your Tesla, or if you can read articles from different sources in one place, like on Facebook. The brand that screams the loudest no longer receives the most of the attention. It is the one that offers something genuinely useful that does.

(g) Communicate more about the EU's role in the world

This is an effective way to involve the citizens of Europe themselves. However, more resources need to be allocated to achieve this. European institutions should also recognise that there is an external aspect which is very important. It is the role of the Union in the world. Communicating that aspect will also reinforce internal communication inside the EU. There is a tendency towards myopia in the field of external communication that is not in Europe's own best interests. The EU fails to deliver when it comes to communication at a global level. For example, while the rest of the world was trying to make sense of the euro crisis, the bulk of the EU's communication budget was spent on the member states.

Europe needs to challenge the myths that surround the bloc by presenting stories that answer citizens' concerns. The EU needs a real communication revolution if it wants to highlight its achievements and its added value. However, branding, PR, or communication cannot work properly if not backed by real reforms and political will. All communication strategies start with policy, they start with performance, they start with action. Most of the problems of the EU, including Euroscepticism and populism, can be tackled if the Union itself begins to change, perform better, and is seen to be doing so by EU citizens.

Crisis communications, nation branding, public communication, PR: the coronavirus crisis is an example of how not to do it. Governments and institutions need to constantly reinforce public trust and enhance their reputation via their communications on how they are successfully managing the rising complications of this global crisis. There's much to be learned from crisis communication best practices, but there is also a lot we can learn from seeing organisations doing it wrong. Analysing their mistakes can help us avoid making similar ones.

The founding fathers of the Union shared the same desire for the pacification of Europe, not via a balance of power, as was the case after the Vienna Congress in 1815, but via the reconciliation and integration of European nations. They wanted a strong, united, and prosperous Europe.

Despite the slow unification process we have seen over the last seven decades in Europe, divisions are widening even more lately because of COVID-19. On the other hand, as long as humanity as a whole undergoes the same traumatic experiences repeatedly there will be, gradually, a larger sense of unity. However, this will be a slower process than the rise of nationalism.

I strongly believe that the European Union allows us to preserve our welfare-state model of society, our liberal democracies, and the diversity of our national cultures. By joining forces and working together we can find workable solutions to many issues. A politically unified Europe is the best remedy against the rise of poverty, alt-right, intolerance, and racism.

Even after losing Britain, the EU remains one of the main players on the planet despite its very slow decision process. If we want to play an important role and have some influence on the international political agenda and the solution of global problems, we must keep our forces together. Europe is the best solution to address the issues we face, even if the politicians fail to explain so to their citizens. Abandoning European unification would be equal to quitting the world stage for good.

Chapter 8

The Identity Crisis

European identity, it seems, is only perceived by educated people. And that is sad, but it is a start.

— Umberto Eco

A fun map from 2014 suggests twenty different ways to divide Europe based on cultural habits and traditions. There is butter Europe and olive oil Europe; tea Europe and coffee Europe; tomato Europe and potato Europe. But, as the Brexit referendum highlighted, the biggest current division in Europe is the one between its cosmopolitan and national identities.

On 6 May 2017, the European Parliament opened the House of European History in Brussels. This museum will delve into the topic of European identity, a concept that predates the European Union itself. A permanent exhibition – in all 24 of the EU's official languages – shows the timeline of European history beginning with the 19th century, leading visitors through the events of the 20th century and ending with a search for a better, united Europe after the World Wars.

Research suggests that many EU citizens don't view their national identity and a bigger European one as being mutually exclusive. Identification with Europe does exist, but it is a complex phenomenon framed in several ways and does not necessarily imply support for the EU. So, European identities are not necessarily mutually exclusive with national identities.

The outcome of the UK's 2016 referendum on EU membership sent shockwaves across Europe. Among other impacts, it has prompted debates around the issue as to whether a "European identity" actually exists or whether national identities still dominate. There are different reasons for the actual identity crisis in Europe. The three most important are:

- Nationalism, populism, and the division between North, South, and East.
- The EU's failure to be a more democratic and social Europe.
- The euro crisis and the refugee problem.

Nationalism, populism, and the division between North, South, and East

Nationalist and populist movements that arose after the financial crisis of 2008 mostly portray immigrants as the source of anxiety, economic problems, and social disorder. They create a perception that immigrants are taking all the jobs that were destined for natives. The financial crisis gave young Europeans a very tough time. They face many obstacles and challenges, much more so than when I started my career almost thirty years ago.

From France's Rassemblement National (formerly Front National) and Germany's AfD to Geert Wilders' Party for Freedom (PVV) in the Netherlands, Vlaams Belang in Belgium, Austria's Freedom Party (FPÖ), and the True Finns in Finland, far-right nationalist parties are challenging the status quo all over Europe and disseminating a populist, anti-immigrant message of hate.

The majority of voters of these populist radical right parties are less educated and afraid of losing their national identity. In most of the countries of southern Europe, we have quite the opposite. Parties like Podemos, Syriza in Greece, and the Five Star Movement in Italy tend to attack the system from the populist left. Podemos and Syriza supporters in Spain and Greece, have university degrees and don't seem to be against immigration.

Nevertheless, the above are broad generalisations and every country has its own identity and past. The difference between these two groups has to do with their own experience in the EU. The northern EU member states are more attractive to less wealthy job-seeking migrants. Their contribution to the Union's budget is considerably bigger in comparison with the return they have from Brussels.

A third major player in populism and Europhobia are the so-called Visegrad Group which receive a considerable amount of money from the EU budget and at the same time are Europhobic as they believe that the Union harms their sovereignty and national identity. Countries like Poland and Hungary are finding it difficult to distance themselves of their autocratic and undemocratic political heritage.

Poland has been plunged into a deep political crisis by its conservative government raising questions about the ruling party's commitment to democracy. Fears are running high in Europe that Poland and other EU countries could be on a path similar to that of Hungary. Viktor Orban has centralised power and restricted civil liberties in creating a so-called "illiberal state".

Despite their diversity, the different forms of Euroscepticism and Europhobia converge towards populist rhetoric. The general features of populism are relatively easy to identify: political, economic, and social denunciation of the elites accused of having stolen power and betrayed the people; political introversion; and fear of immigration. They all undermine EU's political project without offering any concrete suggestions for a common European future.

The European identity can be defined as a number of values shared by all the citizens living in the European Union. Today, the EU is characterised by two opposing trends: one which emphasises the importance of national identities; and the other that advocates the right to a common identity and a cosmopolitan culture.

The EU has funded a number of programmes to research the EU identity issue. Two of the most interesting are EUCROSS and COHESIFY. The EUCROSS project mapped Europeans' cross-national experiences, such as living or travelling in Europe or knowing someone in or from another

European country, and sought to measure "transnationalism". According to the project coordinator Ettore Recchi, based at the University of Chieti-Pescara, while this term is often used in reference to migrants, the European project is making everyone transnational to some extent. The project was designed to find out whether these experiences contribute to a European identity, a "we" feeling. If people identify with Europe, this will lead to a more unified, integrated Europe than a sum of different nations and nationalities following national interests as a primary goal.

EUCROSS assessed identification with Europe, support for the EU, solidarity with other Europeans, and cosmopolitanism. The EUCROSS project found that cross-border experiences have led to a widespread sense of living in a multicultural and borderless society. Instead of focusing on creating an identity, policymakers should defend mobility which, in the long run, will pay off in terms of social integration.

COHESIFY was a multidisciplinary project funded by the EU's Horizon 2020 research programme. It investigated the impact of the EU Cohesion Policy on citizens' identification with Europe at the regional level. This policy is the EU's strategy to promote and support the overall harmonious development of its member states and regions. An original and representative survey was conducted with the participation of more than 8,500 citizens in 17 regions across 12 EU member states, which vary considerably in terms of Cohesion Policy allocations, attitudes to the EU, political-institutional conditions, and economic development.

Overall, the findings provide clear evidence of the positive impact of Cohesion Policy on European identity. The perceived economic benefits of Cohesion Policy for individual's daily lives and for their region's development also contribute to European identity. Additionally, the more individuals are exposed to EU media, such as *Euronews* which extensively covers developments in both EU and member states' politics, the more they are likely to put the EU first in terms of their identity. In other words, the Cohesion Policy improves the recognition of the advantages of the EU and EU integration.

The EU's failure to create a more democratic and social Europe

In an interview with *The Wall Street Journal* on 24 February 2012, Mario Draghi, president of the European Central Bank, declared that the European social model is gone.

> "There are no quick fixes to Europe's problems. Continuing economic shocks would force countries into structural changes in labour markets and other aspects of the economy, to return to long-term prosperity. There was a time when German economist Rudi Dornbusch used to say that the Europeans are so rich they can afford to pay everybody for not working. That's gone," he said.

Since 2008, key elements of the European social model have been radically transformed and sometimes dismantled in some EU member states – even though they were clearly not the cause of the crisis or the budgetary deficits. The European social model is struggling after the adoption of fiscal consolidation reforms during the financial and economic crisis.

It played a vital role in shaping European societies after the Second World War by promoting inclusive economic growth, high living standards, and fair working conditions. It is based on the common vision that many EU member states have for a society that combines economic growth with social cohesion. It emerged during the 1950s thanks to cheap energy, new technologies, and market liberalisation. The European social model also enjoyed a low degree of external competition as China and India were at the time small actors in the global economy.

In the book *Unwrapping the European social model* (2006), Maria Jespen and Amparo Serrano Pascual, indicate that

> "the use of the concept of the European social model in academic and political debate is characterised by two main and

interconnected features: on the one hand, the usually taken-for-granted assumption of the reality of the concept – the reality called 'Europe' becomes a naturally occurring phenomenon – on the other hand, the highly ambiguous and polysemic nature of this concept."

The response of the EU to the financial crisis of 2008 was different from the US. Consisting of a combination of fiscal austerity, neoliberal structural reforms, and expansionary monetary policies it appears to have failed. Eight years after the outbreak of the financial crisis, the overall real GDP of the eurozone in 2016 was still below the pre-crisis peak at the beginning of 2008. According to *Social Europe* (2016) this was the case for the Greek economy which showed a 27.6% contraction. Spain and Portugal were 4.5% and 6.5% lower, respectively.

The most significant problem facing young people in Europe is not terrorism, Brexit, migration, or even climate change. For 81% of the participants in Politico's (12.08.2016) first Youth Caucus, the top concerns are youth unemployment and lack of economic growth. During the last years, we have seen the European social model under increasing threat. A less social Europe has led to social injustice on an unprecedented scale, massive inequities, and a loss of trust in the established political elites.

The social impact of globalisation in Europe is also an important dimension of the EU identity crisis. It is evident that globalisation is having a significant influence on the economic and societal developments of this century. The international flow of capital, services, and products has increased, especially over the last two decades. One of the most important aspects of globalisation is that countries such as China and India have reintegrated into the global economy after decades of isolation. Together with the reintegration of former communist countries in Europe, they made the supply of cheap labour available at a global level, and increased the number of consumers and the size and diversity of the potential market for EU export.

In 2007, Jain Begg, Juraj Draxler, and Jorgen Mortensen described the consequences of globalisation for the European social model in their report *Is Social Europe Fit for Globalisation? A study on the social impact of globalisation in the European Union*:

> "These trends have been associated with growing prosperity in aggregate, but it is clear that there are losers as well as winners. In particular, rapid advances in technology, coupled with adjustments in some global markets have exerted pressures on the returns to unskilled labour in Europe, with the falling relative wages of unskilled workers contributing to a widening of income inequalities. Against this backdrop, there have been growing fears that the European social model, seen as a defining feature of the European Union and its member states, can no longer be sustained and that it will have to be reined-back or even dismantled."

As former European Commission president Jacques Delors underlines in his foreword in David Rinaldi's report, *A new start for social Europe*: "if European policy-making jeopardises cohesion and sacrifices social standards, there is no chance for the European project to gather support from European citizens".

This report, published in February 2016, and commissioned by the Ministry of Labour, Employment, and the Social and Solidarity Economy of Luxembourg, focuses on the necessity for a new start for Social Europe. It identifies three pillars on which the Social Europe project should be grounded:

- An investment strategy in human capital, which will set the basis for growth and competitiveness based on social inclusion and resilience.
- An enhanced and fairer labour mobility across EU member states to build a real European labour market.

- A pro-convergence reform of European economic governance, which would reconcile social and macroeconomic objectives.

Social Europe has been a source of inspiration for several emerging economies like Morocco, Brazil, and China. It is now crucial that the Union expresses strong opinions and adopts the necessary decisions for preserving the social model that has played such a pivotal role in its history.

The Euro crisis

In 2007, EU economies seemed to be doing relatively well, with positive economic growth and low inflation, but two years after its appearance, the 2008 global financial crisis was transformed into the eurozone crisis in 2010. Several eurozone member states like Greece, Portugal, Spain, Cyprus, and Ireland, were unable to repay, or refinance their government debt or bail out their over-debt banks. Some countries have now been in a depression for years, while the governing powers of the eurozone have been going from emergency to emergency, most particularly in Greece.

The European debt crisis also severely dented the credibility of the EU and created a large crisis concerning common identity. In May 2012, Mario Draghi, the head of the European Central Bank (ECB), declared that the crisis had exposed the inadequacy of the financial and economic framework set up for the euro monetary union launched in 1999. The euro was supposed to bring convergence to EU economies, yet it seems that it has caused even greater divergence. To discourage governments from expecting more EU bailouts, the emphasis on austerity might have been politically necessary when the debt crisis began. Nevertheless, this policy has also brought EU growth close to zero, encouraged deflation and unemployment, fed exasperation across the continent and led to the impoverishment of large parts of the Greek population and other eurozone countries like Spain, Italy, and Portugal.

The IMF, the ECB, and the European Commission formed the so-called troika, which intervened in 2010 to keep Athens from defaulting on its debts and having to leave the eurozone. Greece was placed under a system of forced administration. In 2013, the IMF admitted that it made major mistakes on the first bailout, setting excessively optimistic expectations for the country's economy and underestimating the effects of the austerity actions it imposed. The rescue package kept the country afloat, but it came in exchange for exaggerated austerity measures that have deepened recession and encouraged extremist political parties and polarisation.

In July 2016, the IMF's handling of the financial crisis in the eurozone was criticised by the Independent Evaluation Office (IEO), the organisation's own independent watchdog in a report which stated that the fund had failed to identify the scale of the problem. According to the report, the IMF was guilty of over-optimistic forecasts and left the impression that it was treating EU countries in a different way. While accepting that solving the problems of Ireland, Greece, and Portugal posed extraordinary challenges, the IMF's Independent Evaluation Office (IEO) said the fund had missed the build-up of banking system risks in some countries and shared the widely held "Europe is different" mindset. The report looked into how the IMF handled the eurozone crisis, which began with the bailout of Greece in May 2010 and spread to Ireland, Portugal, and Cyprus. On his blog, Varoufakis called the report of the IMFa "brutal assessment, leaving no room for doubt about the vulgar economics and the gunboat diplomacy employed by the troika".

Before the UK referendum of 23 June 2016, European Council President Donald Tusk told the German newspaper *Bild* of his "fear that Brexit could, in fact, be the start of the process of destruction of not only the EU but also of Western political civilization". Although Brexit appears a big threat for the EU, it is the euro, and how it is constructed today, that forms probably a much bigger menace for the future of Europe.

In his book *The Euro: How a Common Currency Threatens the Future of Europe* (2016), Joseph Stiglitz, the Nobel laureate economist, describes the euro as a tragic mistake, a currency begun without the necessary political integration or clear thinking about its fundamental flaws. In theory, the best choice for Europe would be to forge ahead to full fiscal union, essentially creating a United States of Europe, argues Stiglitz. But because "there is more than a small probability that it will not be done," he proposes various ways that Europe could escape from a halfway-in, halfway-out agony.

The refugee problem

More than a million migrants and refugees came to Europe in 2015, creating a crisis as the EU member states struggled to cope with the influx, and creating division over how best to deal with resettling people. The International Organization for Migration (IOM) reported that an estimated 204,311 migrants and refugees entered Europe by sea in 2016 from 1 January to 30 May, arriving in Italy, Greece, Cyprus, and Spain. Most of the migrants and refugees arrived from countries in conflict like Syria, Iraq, and Afghanistan. In September 2016, EU ministers voted by a majority to relocate 160,000 refugees EU-wide, but Hungary rejected this plan. For the time being the plan could only apply to those who are in Italy and Greece.

Tensions in the EU have been rising because of the disproportionate burden faced by some countries. This was the case especially in Greece and Italy as well as Austria, where the majority of migrants were landing. Border closures in Central and Eastern Europe and the March 2016 deal with Turkey led to a significant decline in arrivals of migrants and asylum seekers by sea to Greece compared to 2015. The migration from North Africa to Italy kept pace with previous years. As Ankara hinted in May – only two months later – it may just let the whole arrangement collapse, a step that could again send refugees streaming across the Aegean; Europe has quietly begun preparing a Plan B.

According to *Politico*, Brussels' contingency plan, described by senior diplomats, envisions turning Greece into a giant refugee camp. The whole idea of the deal with Turkey was to keep refugees from being stranded in Greece as it does not have the capacity to deal with an influx that could quickly reach the hundreds of thousands. But with many European countries refusing to accept more than a symbolic number of migrants, this could become an option that many Greeks fear. EU countries have shown themselves unable to deliver a solution to the refugee crisis under the current rules and it is precisely their inability to develop a shared approach that is making the emergency so hard to control.

In the following years, Turkey often threatened to terminate the agreement because the visa freedom for Turkish citizens provided for under the agreement had not yet been implemented. Ankara repeatedly used this deal to blackmail the EU, threatening to re-open its borders, while six billion euros were granted to Turkey for the 3.7 million refugees in its territory. Then, in February 2020, the Turkish government decided unilaterally to suspend the 2016 EU–Turkey deal and tens of thousands of refugees were sent by Ankara to the Greek borders. This manufactured crisis turned people in need of safety and dignity into political bargaining chips. As Eric Reidy notes in the New Humanitarian of 4 March 2020:

"Since it was signed, the agreement has created a years-long humanitarian crisis on the Greek islands and turned refugees into a bargaining chip wielded by Turkish President Recip Tayyip Erdogan to extract support and policy concessions from the EU, according to refugee advocates, and human rights groups."

"Since Turkey announced it would open its borders, thousands of refugees hoping to reach Europe have travelled – sometimes with apparent help from the Turkish government and in the full glare of frontline media coverage of a once-clandestine activity – to Edirne, a Turkish city close to the border with Greece and Bulgaria, and to the Turkish coast."

Chapter 9

The Rise of Illiberal Democracy

La démocratie, ce n'est pas la loi de la majorité, mais la protection de la minorité.

— Albert Camus

Around 25 years ago, CNN's Fareed Zakaria wrote an essay in foreign affairs titled "The Rise of Illiberal Democracy". His thesis was that democracies around the world were surrendering to illiberal reforms, and that the strands holding the traditions of democracy and liberalism together were rapidly eroding.

> "From Peru to the Palestinian Authority, from Sierra Leone to Slovakia, from Pakistan to the Philippines," he wrote, "we see the rise of a disturbing phenomenon in international life – illiberal democracy."

Zakaria's article made an important distinction between democracy and liberalism, constructs that are often conflated. Democracy is a process for choosing leaders; it's about popular participation. To say that a state is democratic is to say little about how it is actually governed.

Liberalism, by contrast, is about the norms and practices that shape political life. A properly liberal state is one in which individual rights are paramount. It protects the individual against the abuses of a tyrant and the abuses of democratic majorities.

The illiberal trend the journalist noted in 1997 has accelerated. New members have since joined the club of Pakistan and the Philippines such as Brazil and the EU's Hungary and Poland. The Western world isn't becoming less democratic, but it is becoming less liberal. Even more alarming, what was a trend is now an increasingly fixed reality.

In the Eurasia Group's report on the world's top risks for 2016, Ian Bremmer and Cliff Kupchan argued that the different realities inside the EU would reach a critical point as an identity crisis emerged between open Europe and closed Europe. A combination of inequality, refugees, terrorism, and grassroots political pressures pose a fundamental challenge to the principles on which the European Union was found. Well, we are there.

"Open Europe" refers to the Europe that German Chancellor Angela Merkel stands for: it's open to the world and the borders between EU member states are open to one another. "Closed Europe" is the Europe of Orban and most of the Visegrad countries. It is the continent of isolationism that collectively closes itself up from the outside world, while each individual country closes itself up from others.

In 2020 we definitely experienced the conflict between Poland and Hungary on one side and the rest of the EU concerning rule of law issues. As Alberto Allemano, EU law professor at HEC Business School in Paris, stated:

> "2020 has revealed the fragility of the rule of law underpinning the Union's democratic life. This self-inflicted, complacent erosion of rule of law is inevitably set to affect the EU's ambition to self-sufficiency. The Union can't appear as a democracy when it no longer acts as one".

The culture of Brussels bashing

A variety of factors negatively influence the further unification of the EU such as globalisation, the financial crisis, austerity, the European identity crisis, Brexit, the rule of law concerns in Hungary and Poland, the lack of transparency in the EU Council and low media interest. Nevertheless, one of the main reasons that further unification in the EU fails is the tendency among European politicians to portray the Union as a faceless monster which is the cause of everything that goes wrong on the continent.

Politicians who want to make themselves popular and interesting blame the EU. Added to this is the schizophrenic behaviour of European heads of state and governments. On the one hand, they go to Brussels to participate in summits, make political decisions, and on the other hand, often go back to their countries and blame the EU for those decisions. Bottom line: some EU countries receive billions of euros from Brussels while their governments tell lies to their citizens concerning the decisions taken inside the Council of the EU.

One good example of such behaviour is the Hungarian PM Orban. In April 2017, he launched an initiative called "Let's stop Brussels", only days after European leaders gathered in Rome to mark the EU's 60th anniversary. In February 2019, the Hungarian press reported that Orban had written a letter to his compatriots, saying that "Brussels has learned nothing from the terrible terrorist attacks of recent years and wants to bring more immigrants to Europe". The European Commission reacted strongly to this new anti-immigration campaign launched by the Hungarian PM by saying it "distorts the truth" and refuting most of its points. This was quite unusual because the EU's communication policy about disinformation and fake news was deplorable until a few years ago. For example, the European Commission did not react during the Brexit referendum campaign, when false claims were being made about the EU and the UK's relationship with the Union.

Since the global financial and economic crisis of 2007–08 and the start of the debt crisis in 2010, it has become fashionable to pick on the EU and hold it responsible, not only for its own mistakes but also for other problems not of its doing. Less competent politicians help the transfer of mistrust by bashing Europe or their neighbouring countries to reinforce their electoral base.

In January 2019, European Ombudsman, Emily O'Reilly, welcomed the European Parliament's strong vote of support for her recommendations to improve the transparency and accountability of EU national governments' legislative work in Brussels.

> "The lack of legislative transparency in the Council of the EU has allowed the 'blame Brussels' culture to endure for far too long. I hope today's vote will help convince national governments to

agree to make EU law-making more open, so the public can see who is really making the decisions," said Ms O'Reilly.

"This will require a culture change in the Council, away from old-style diplomacy where much is kept hidden, to a more open, and democratic way of working. Taking no action would further damage EU democracy, as this crucial part of the EU legislative process is not open to citizens."

"It would be unthinkable at the national level for Ministers not to tell citizens their positions on national legislation. However this is essentially what happens when the same Ministers meet to decide on EU legislation," said the Ombudsman.

Most EU countries place their own interests before the general one. In Hungary and Poland, lawmakers have increased their anti-Brussels rhetoric. In November 2020, both countries even blocked the EU budget and the coronavirus relief plan over an EU clause linking the funds to the rule of law.

The rhetoric from Warsaw and Budapest has been outrageous. The Polish government rambled on and on about being "enslaved" by the European Union because it wants to interfere in Polish internal matters. Meanwhile, Hungarian Prime Minister Viktor Orban has been taking things even further, comparing the EU with the Soviet Union for the regulations it wants to impose on his country. The veto on the €1.8 trillion budget by Hungary and Poland has catapulted the EU back into crisis mode. Finding an agreement on the COVID-19 recovery plan was not easy. However, the EU has itself to blame: it passively stood by as first Hungary, then Poland, setting up authoritarian structures.

Budapest has shown how a couple of oligarchs can hand the Orban government an almost total stranglehold on the media using a long-term plan implemented during the last few years. The same thing happened with the dismantling of the independent judiciary. Every year, new legislation was passed that further restricted the freedom of the country's judges until finally the government was in control. In response, Brussels took Hungary to the European Court of Justice.

In the case of Poland, the European Commission requested EU action in December 2017 given the perceived threats to the independence of the judiciary. In a resolution adopted in March 2018, the European Parliament agreed with the Commission on the risks to the rule of law in Poland.

In September 2018, the European Parliament voted to trigger Article 7 disciplinary procedures against Hungary for undermining democratic rules. It requested that the Council acts to prevent the Hungarian authorities from breaching the EU's founding values. MEPs were chiefly concerned about judicial independence, freedom of expression, corruption, rights of minorities, and the situation of migrants and refugees.

Article 7 of the Treaty on European Union is a procedure in the treaties of the European Union (EU) to suspend certain rights from a member state. While rights can be suspended, there is no mechanism to expel a member. A proposal to trigger Article 7 can be brought by the European Parliament, the EC, or one-third of member states. With the European Parliament's consent, the Council must then reach a four-fifths majority decision on the proposal and speak to the state in question. Once adopted, the measure has two parts – a preventative mechanism and a sanctioning mechanism. Article 7(1), as triggered against Hungary, means a formal warning is given to the state. If this doesn't have the desired effect, Article 7(2) can be used to impose sanctions and suspend EU voting rights. However, nothing substantial happened.

A resolution was adopted in January 2020 noting that reports and statements by the Commission, the UN, OSCE, and the Council of Europe indicate that "the situation in both Poland and Hungary has deteriorated since the triggering of Article 7(1)". MEPs have pointed out that Council hearings under Article 7 of the Treaty are neither regular nor structured. They called on the Council to address concrete recommendations to the countries concerned, including deadlines, to ensure EU law is respected. "The failure by the Council to make effective use of Article 7 continues to undermine the integrity of common European values, mutual trust and the credibility of the European Union as a whole," claimed the European Parliament.

Despite the actions of the European Parliament and the EC, most EU countries ignored the conflict. It became obvious that even when the main institutions in Brussels try to do their job well, it comes finally to the Heads of State in the EU Council to take the final decisions – most of the time in a spirit of tribalism, clientelism, and vote-buying. In the meantime, the European Commission has tried to underline the problem in its recent communications:

> "Member States often promote only their domestic approaches as a basis for European rules, which can lead to political tensions. This, in turn, leads to repeated calls on the Commission to come forward with new ideas, but the willingness to follow through is not guaranteed." (*The Single Market in a changing world*, 22.11.2018).

> "Member States have used sovereignty and unanimity as the basis for their arguments to protect specific national interests to the detriment of the Single Market. [...] This often makes member states overly cautious, dampening ambitions, and weakening the final outcome." (*Towards a more efficient and democratic decision making in EU tax policy*, 15.01.2019).

> "When national rule of law safeguards do not seem capable of addressing threats to the rule of law in a Member State, it is a common responsibility of the EU institutions and the member states to take action to remedy the situation. As well as the common

obligation to defend EU values, there is a common interest in tackling issues such as threats to Constitutional Courts or judicial independence before they can compromise the implementation of EU law, policies, or funding." (Further strengthening the rule of law within the Union State of play and possible next steps, 03.04.2019).

The EU blame game, whether it takes place in the UK, the Netherlands, Germany, or France, is rarely followed by a concrete vision of what should replace the EU we know. What is even worse is that it reinforces the pattern of negativism in media coverage. It results in negative framing, Euroscepticism, and popular editorial EU-bashing and, seems to mix up who the EU actually is. If you ask politicians and commentators in the news, they often blame Brussels rather than the national capitals for the malaise of Europe.

Nevertheless, a good alternative for change could be the upcoming Conference on the Future of Europe. It could provide an excellent opportunity for EU institutions to take stock of citizens' views and communicate the European project accurately.

Chapter 10

Is the Medium Really the Message?

The new electronic independence re-creates the world in the image of a global village.

— Marshall McLuhan

"The medium is the message" is a phrase coined by communications theorist Marshall McLuhan back in 1964. He tried to explain that the form media takes actually embeds itself in the message and influences how that message is perceived. In his book *Understanding the Media: The Extensions of Man,* he states that:

> "In a culture like ours, long accustomed to splitting and dividing all things as a means of control, it is sometimes a bit of a shock to be reminded that, in operational, and practical fact, the medium is the message. This is merely to say that the personal and social consequences of any medium – that is, of any extension of our-selves – result from the new scale that is introduced into our affairs by each extension of ourselves, or by any new technology."

In 1964, McLuhan was right. Messages that reached audiences through radio or TV were perceived differently than messages that came through print. McLuhan maintained that the ways the messages were delivered were, in fact, a part of the message. And that is absolutely right. The medium can be the message itself if it delivers content that would otherwise be impossible to access.

But he was also wrong. Born in 1911 and passing away in 1980, McLuhan had no opportunity to experience the Internet the way we know it today. There were no websites. There was no email. Nobody was writing blogs. There was no Facebook or Twitter. Even so, that didn't stop him from exerting a huge influence on digital media. It was McLuhan who first spoke about technology and communication having the ability to create a "global village".

As an early pioneer of the study of communication and its evolution over time, McLuhan introduced many observations about the impact of new forms of communications and media. Today, however, we sometimes have the impression that because we have posted something on our website, or sent out an email, or posted a blog, or sent out a tweet, that we have communicated. As George Bernard Shaw famously said: "The single biggest problem in communication is the illusion that it has taken place".

Your medium is not always your message. Your PC, laptop, smartphone, the Internet, social media platforms do not communicate. They are just tools, and you may not be communicating the message you think you are. Since the early days of communication, humanity has been captivated by its methods to deliver and preserve information. How we communicate with each other defines who we are. How we communicate makes a culture and an individual unique.

The miracle of communication

Effective communication is important in both personal and professional aspects of our lives, particularly as ineffective communication can create short- and long-term issues. Many organisations often do not think about communicating while doing it but concentrate on how sending and receiving information might eliminate problems and improve relationships.

Communication is effective if everything in the communication process goes as planned, and when the recipient understands the message in the way the sender intended. As the EU has increased the range of its political responsibilities and the number of member states within quite a short period, communication has become more complicated.

Although citizens initially approved European integration, their scepticism has grown simultaneously with the ongoing engagement with political issues by the EU during the last years. Distrust and passivity peaked in 2005 with the rejection of the referendums on the European Constitution in France and the Netherlands; again in 2009 and 2014 with the lowest participation ever in the European elections; and finally, in 2016, with the discharge of EU membership by the British.

Today, communication disruption is present in all organisations – private and government; unilateral and multilateral. Digital technology is rapidly disrupting institutions and corporations. New technologies and innovative start-ups emerge every day. Simply put: the balance of power has changed. The reputation of a brand can be severely damaged in minutes. Brand loyalty, reputation, credibility, and trust are increasingly influenced by people's experiences.

Public communication is one of the most challenging and sensitive issues in contemporary democracies. The commitment of the EU to multilingualism is often accused of being one of the obstacles for integration. Some politicians and theorists think that one common lingua franca would be a magnificent solution, to allow a better participation to all EU citizens. The language issue and having one language – although in our days a utopian perspective – is not the only gap between citizens and the Brussels bubble.

Winston Churchill one said that the difference between poor management and leadership is communication. During the Second World War, the radio was one of the few media for transmitting messages directly to the public. With his charisma and outstanding communication skills, the British prime minister managed to mobilise not only his own country but the whole world. When he spoke, millions of citizens listened and supported him in his campaign against fascism, intolerance, and discrimination. He gave hope to the people around the globe. His messages were clear, consistent, and honest. He never lied about the sacrifices that were needed to win the war. Churchill communicated in a transparent manner and furnished a comprehensible long-term vision. His determination and the authenticity of his message made him trustworthy and a key person of influence.

Know your audience

Many factors play a disadvantageous role and make public communication more difficult. They include lack of leadership; absence of a shared vision and a common European public sphere; poor knowledge on the

EU; hostile media; EU red tape; unethical practices in politics; the blame game on Europe; and the EU's inability to communicate transparently and fairly its policies and achievements. All these elements form significant communication discrepancies for the EU and undermine its future. In addition, not all Europeans are interested in important news about politics, economy, or foreign affairs.

Today's audiences are central to the success of an organisation or a project. Peopleno longer accept being "talked at". EU communication is too often based on one-way informational messages rather than genuine dialogue. Governments should realise that they don't have the last say any longer in creating policies. Global connectivity continues its unparalleled progression, and many old institutions will have to adapt or become irrelevant to modern society.

The EU should invest more in attracting communication professionals, in the training and education of its communicators, and a sustainable relationship with the press. Inside the EU, communication itself is often considered a secondary task proceeding from the administrative staff and often subjected to it. As a result, any communications project is essentially focused on management and is too self-centred.

Organisations in the public sector need more communication professionals, and by communication professionals, I mean people who have accredited qualifications and expertise and experience in the private sector. There remains much to be done in order to transfer skills and expertise from the private to the public sector.

Many communication officers and spokespersons are former journalists. The background in journalism of EU staff in communication positions appears to reflect the presumption that public communication is equivalent to media relations and is somehow linked to a tactical communication approach. Employing communication professionals from a broader range of communication backgrounds including communication scientists and public relations experts would be advantageous.

The media play an important role and have an impact on the public opinion, as information concerning the EU is mainly provided by national and local media, which is primarily TV. A European public sphere does not really exist and the citizens are only informed about the EU by their national media in each country. Besides this, the EU does not have any charismatic leaders, it is perceived as faceless, and news about it does not always find a connection with the daily lives of the people. If news about the Union could be framed in terms of EU membership benefits and offering solutions to real European problems, their effectiveness would improve and their perception made more positive.

To be successful, via the press or other channels, the European message needs to be interesting to the media and citizens. It needs the kind of storytelling that captures their interest. Storytelling is persuasive and moves people. The desire to share and consume stories appears to be just as instinctive. We tell stories during our whole life and there is not a day on the entire planet that is not touched by a story. Humans are wired to listen to stories, to tell stories, and to love stories.

Over the last few years, the terms "content marketing" and "content strategy" became buzzwords in the corporate world and media. Content marketing is the art of producing and disseminating relevant and useful content to attract, entertain, and engage a clearly defined target audience to promote products or services. Organisations that realise the influence clients and stakeholders possess in shaping brands will succeed. And those who actively engage in conversations with them will consolidate their reputation and earn trust.

The opinion of the experts

What will the world look like once this corona crisis is under control? What will change on our planet, and what will remain the same? Many organisations are rethinking their communications strategies.

I asked an open question to a group of communication professionals:

"How would communications look in a post corona era? What will stay and what will change?"

This is what they had to say:

> "In the not for profit sector, we were used to communicating about crises occurring abroad and Western audiences were called to act for the others, to support them facing 'their' Ebola outbreak, 'their' earthquake or famine. In the 80s, "We are the world" was written in support of Ethiopians facing a huge nutritional crisis, today Lady Gaga's "One world: together at home" live stream concert was organised to praise "all of the medical workers that are putting their lives at risk for us". A new sense of proximity and collective responsibility will require a paradigm shift to expand the "together at home" concept in ways to respond to people's need to feel reassured by their protective domestic environment and the need to continue being a social animal."
>
> Sergio Cecchini, Director Communication & Fundraising,
> Médecins Sans Frontières, Belgium

> "In the brave new post corona world everything will change. It is up to us to ensure that change is for the better. It can only be positive if 'equality' is at the heart and soul of the transformation. That means placing social, environmental, and economic policy on an equal footing. It's called the theory of SOC/EN/OMICS and it means putting health before wealth, conservation before consumption, and community before cost. Above all, it means communicating a new message that everyone can understand and enjoy."
>
> Jane Morrice, former Vice President European Economic & Social Committee (EESC), responsible for communications, EU

"For decades, messaging, and communication tactics, aided by technological advances, have continually lurched from the collective to the personal. The COVID-19 pandemic, however, has exposed and reminded us of our shared responsibilities and future. It's difficult not to notice in public opinion research that concerns for public health and the economy at-large are outranking concerns for personal health and finance. I believe this is less a departure from individualist thinking, but rather a heightened sense of how our individual decisions and their consequences affect others. How long this reorientation will last is yet to be seen, but communicators should note, and plan for it."

Michael Dabbs, Senior Communications Officer,
The Gill Foundation, US

"The communications function will have an absolutely vital role to play during and after the pandemic on four fronts: (a) Keeping the organisation and its ecosystem cohesive and engaged during prolonged periods of remote working (b) Shaping the narrative of the company during a period of intense change (c) Ensuring that the product and service portfolio of the company remains relevant to the current and changed needs of clients and (d) Building up new capabilities – e.g. ability to do virtual events, stronger content play through social media, digital channels – to ensure the company's brand, reputation, and relationships keep strengthening rather than weakening during this period. Just like fire departments prove their importance in times of arson, communications teams come alive during crises. Those that can help their companies and CEOs negotiate this crisis by reinventing themselves and adding value at every stage of the lockdown and reopening, will find themselves becoming more core and important in the scheme of things to their businesses and leadership teams."

Abhinav Kumar, Chief Marketing & Communications
Officer – Global Markets, TATA, Belgium

"Economy and consumers will change. But communication will not. For me, the keyword is "acceleration", not "change". The Internet has profoundly changed communication: new channels... new rules. But COVID-19 will accelerate the communication trends well known to communicators. We will see brands that are more authentic, that play a social role, [more] transparent and closer to the real interests of their stakeholders (workers first!) in digital ways. Not just storytelling, but story-doing. And, above all, more agile, and flexible in their strategy and action. One headline: 'Accelerate your communication from values and purpose. Contribute, be digital, stay agile'."

Fuencisla Cid Rodríguez, Communication
Director EOSA, Spain

"I believe communications post-corona crisis would evolve, transform and change as organisations and employees had to adjust to new teleworking environments and social distancing measures during these very difficult times. The world will be even more hyper-connected, virtual communications, and video calls will increase, maximising the communications exchange among individuals and business. Also, new fact-checking organisations, and jobs in the disinformation field will arise to monitor, validate, and contrast the validity and veracity of information published on digital media and social media platforms. However, one-to-one communication will prevail."

Alba Perez Grandi, Communications Team Leader, European
Union Agency for Cybersecurity (ENISA), EU

"The volume of news we perceive during the pandemic already exceeds a million times every other crisis event in our present-day life. This has proven that communicators' capacity to have even more advanced digital instruments to manage and analyse data remains a core subject in our profession and we will furthermore be discovering the outcomes. I believe the influence of social media in our daily life and fake news generated to support political and private interests will increase. Furthermore these trends will gain dangerous dimensions. In the new era after the virus, my faith is in the young generation, their professional values and qualities to run for an ethically informed society."

Manuela Toteva, Account Manager, Global
Marketing, SAP, Germany

"I always believed that 'a communicator is a hope creator'. So, if there's a thing of which I remain certain, this is that the creation of hope will remain the mainspring of communication. We have clearly seen this during the sanitary crisis and we will always swim on the stream of hope, whatever the waves will be. It seems, however, that for the near future communication will be more centered on the ethics of personal and common responsibility."

Yannis Freris, Corporate Communication & Sustainable
Development, GEFYRA SA, Greece

"I foresee that global and regional migration narratives will be more than ever played on the 'values field'. When narratives on the evolution of communities — cities, regions, states or continents – are heavily polarised, there is no bigger mistake in advocacy than virtue signalling a person's value to the denigration of someone else's. This is what is happening today within migration debates in the free world: A battle of 'best values' instead of 'best arguments' to the detriment of evidence-based policymaking. The analysis of value-based communication will be the biggest breakthrough in policy communication in the social sciences and migration in particular."

Marco Ricorda, Communication Officer at the International
Centre for Migration Policy Development (ICMPD) and
Former Member of Cabinet for the President of the European
Parliament, Antonio Tajani, Italy.

The coronavirus pandemic has made us realise how heavily we depend on digital connectivity. The public is far more engaged and has greater and higher expectations. This is an opportunity for companies to reinforce the public trust and their reputations, respond faster, and adjust their message. Our world post-COVID will be characterised by new human behaviours, industry shifts, and economic disruptions. It will be more digital and will offer many opportunities for marketing and communications to become even more relevant. Across the globe a maximalisation of communication exchange between individuals and businesses will be experienced.

Chapter 11

The New Digital Age

The greatest enemy of knowledge is not ignorance, it is the illusion of knowledge.

— Stephen Hawking

In March 2021, the European Commission presented a "Digital Compass", setting a course for Europe to escape the high-tech malaise and instead produce by 2030 a fifth of the world's semiconductors while also developing its super-fast quantum computer. Nowadays, European semiconductor companies account for 4% of capital investment in a sector dominated by American and Asian giants. At the same time, the EU's largest chipmaker Infineon recently expressed grave doubts about the way ahead.

Reinhard Ploss, who heads this semiconductor offshoot of Siemens, told the *Financial Times* that boosting Europe's smart chips output is probably not the right move. "We had a computer industry…it's gone. We had a consumer electronics industry…it's gone." He suggests that until these sectors are rebuilt within Europe, it makes little sense to plough huge sums into semiconductors, an area where Infineon is an important niche producer but far removed from being one of the big producers worldwide.

According to Giles Merritt, founder of the think tank Friends of Europe, the EU needs a different catch-up strategy. Its thinking doesn't compare well with America's practical approach to sharpening its competitive edge. The investments of the three global giants – Intel in the US, Samsung in South Korea, and Taiwan's TSMC – dwarf those planned in Europe. Infineon's newest semiconductor "foundry" at Villach in Austria costs less than a tenth of TSMC's giant $20bn plant in southern Taiwan. It seems that Europe has missed the microelectronics bus.

In an interview, the former *Financial Times* correspondent uses Aesop's fable "The Hare and the Tortoise" to describe the tech race between the West and China. The hare (the West) is very confident of winning, so it stops during the race and falls asleep. The tortoise (China) continues to move very slowly but finally wins the race without stopping. The moral lesson of the story is that you can be more successful by doing things slowly and steadily than acting quickly and carelessly.

"The first thing we have to do is to be honest with ourselves, To admit how bad the situation is for European technology and how much money we need to invest. The EU Digital Compass is unrealistic. We have to return to where we were 30 years ago in terms of international competition and technology advantage. Europe needs to invest huge amounts of tax money in the style of the French "grand projects" of the 1970s and 1980s where the state intervened in the creation of industrial policy. We are living on fat accumulated in the past years, but it is running out. "We need to be proactive and fix things on time," he said.

Already in 2016, Michael Moritz observed in the *Financial Times* that "Europe's eight most valuable companies are only worth about 10 per cent of Facebook or 6 per cent of Google". A 2019 publication by the European Political Strategy Centre recalls that "while the EU was home to 42 *Fortune 100* businesses in 2007, it boasted only 28 in 2017", and "only 5 of the world's top 100 unicorns – companies with a valuation of over 1 billion US dollars – are from the EU27, with the first only in 56th place".

According to Andrea Renda, Senior Research Fellow at the Centre for European Policy Studies (CEPS), Europe's fear of lagging behind the US and China keeps spreading like an oil slick across the public debate. Commentators point to several factors that would, in their opinion, explain this mounting problem: heavy regulation, lack of venture capital, lack of skills, big government, political unwillingness to complete the single market, and more.

The purchase in 2016 of the German robot manufacturer Kuka by the Chinese company Midea was a blow to high-tech Europe. Since then, Chinese investments in Europe in strategic areas have continued. More surprisingly, China has invested in many European countries to create the world's first electricity grid through its Global Energy Interconnection Initiative, in parallel with its New Silk Road. This network aims to limit its own fossil energy consumption to 50% by 2050 and purchase the remainder externally.

Europe has not been very good at raising technology giants, despite a vibrant start-up environment and some excellent companies in this domain. Europe simply did not create any of those big companies which largely explains the different economic performance of EU and US business over the past decade.

In its publication "Rethinking Strategic Autonomy in the Digital Age", the European Policy Strategy Centre points out that in the 21st century, those who control digital technologies are increasingly able to influence economic, societal, and political outcomes. In this context, the growing "geo-politicisation" of technology implies a paradigm change for the notion of strategic autonomy. Policymakers worldwide are waking up to the critical imprint that digital technologies have on their countries' strategic autonomy, and a global race for technological leadership has ensued. Despite its many assets, the EU is in danger of falling behind in this race. This not only places its long-term economic prosperity at risk, but opens it up to a whole range of strategic vulnerabilities – all the more so against a backdrop of escalating geopolitical tensions.

While staying true to its long-standing commitment to openness, competition, and free, and fair trade, the EU must better understand the new dependencies and vulnerabilities that accompany technological progress and ubiquitous connectivity. It should ensure it has the proper protections in place to deal with them. The EU's ability to defend and promote its interests – as well as its credibility as a strong foreign policy actor – is ever more a function of its cyber resilience and technology leadership.

Artificial intelligence: a curse or a blessing?

Artificial intelligence is rapidly changing the environments of just about everything – from translation to speech recognition, to jobs, to decision-making processes. With its thousands of promised benefits, AI is positioned to affect just about every business around the globe. However, with all the hype surrounding what AI can automate and relieve human be-ings from manually having to do themselves, is AI indeed the blessing it's presented itself to be – or a curse? The question doesn't arise from the scepticism on whether machines will become too intelligent or learn to the point of a robot takeover. While AI is fascinating and the stuff of science fiction, its emergence also raises many concerns, especially in its applications.

The late Stephen Hawking famously expressed his secret fears that AI might one day take over, saying that thinking machines "could spell the end of the human race".' There's irony in his concerns considering that Hawking had to rely on AI to give him the voice that allowed him to interact with the world.

However, Hawking is not the only one who has spoken out on the implica-tions of a world dependent on AI. Anja Kaspersen, former Head of Strategic Engagement and New Technologies at the International Committee of the Red Cross and former Head of Geopolitics and International Security at the World Economic Forum, has been interviewed extensively on her AI views. As a former career diplomat, geo-strategic analyst, and security practitioner, she has dedicated herself to helping governments and inter-national organisations understand and adapt to new innovation waves. On the topic of AI, she talks about its potential to become weaponisable. The US and Chinese militaries are already investing in AI and robotics, and it's unlikely that they will reveal to the public how their AI weapons work. Russia, on the other hand, has already unveiled their "Iron Man" military robot that aims to minimise risk to soldiers.

However, Kaspersen argues that it's not all bad. In an article she wrote on the artificial intelligence arms race, she says,

> "Many AI applications have life-enhancing potential, so holding back its development is undesirable and possibly unworkable. This speaks to the need for a more connected and coordinated

multi-stakeholder effort to create norms, protocols, and mechanisms for the oversight and governance of AI".

Fear of AI is mostly rooted in the lack of knowledge of how others will leverage the technology. With AI intended to automate work and collect data on a massive scale, citizens are concerned about how their data will be managed and who will have access to it. We've reached the point where governments have decided to release directives to regulate AI, as it has become an area of strategic importance and a key driver of economic development. It can bring solutions to many societal challenges, from treating diseases to minimising the environmental impact of farming. However, socioeconomic, legal, and ethical effects must be carefully addressed.

In March 2018, the European Commission opened applications to join an expert group in artificial intelligence which was tasked to:

- Advise the Commission on building a broad and diverse community of stakeholders in a "European AI Alliance".
- Support the implementation of the upcoming European initiative on artificial intelligence (April 2018).
- Propose by the end of the year draft guidelines for the ethical development and use of artificial intelligence based on the EU's fundamental rights.

Furthermore, the European Commission and the member states published a Coordinated action plan on the development of AI in Europe on 7 December 2018 to promote AI development. The EU has also increased its annual investments in AI by 70% under the research and innovation programme Horizon 2020 to approximately 1.5 billion euros for the period 2018–20.

The EU Plan is needed because:

- Only when all European countries work together can they make the most of the opportunities offered by AI and become a world leader in this crucial technology for the future of our societies.

- Europe wants to lead the way in AI-based ethics and shared European values so citizens and businesses can fully trust the technologies they are using.
- Cooperation between member states and the Commission is essential to address new challenges brought by AI.

AI applications bring new ethical and legal questions related to liability or fairness of decision-making. The General Data Protection Regulation (GDPR) is a significant step for building trust and the Commission wants to move a step forward on ensuring legal clarity in AI-based applications. Moreover, in April 2019, the European presented Ethics Guidelines for Trustworthy Artificial Intelligence. This followed the publication of the guidelines' first draft in December 2018 on which more than 500 comments were received through an open consultation.

The EU initiatives are good but are not reaching far enough. AI has made significant steps in the past few years and those rapid advances are raising major ethical dilemmas. For example, a report from the AI Now Institute, an influential research institute based in New York, has identified facial recognition as a critical challenge for society and policymakers. The speed at which facial recognition has grown can be attributed to the rapid development of a type of machine learning known as learning which uses massive tangles of computations – very roughly analogous to the wiring in a biological brain – to recognise data patterns. It is now able to carry out pattern recognition with high accuracy.

How will the EU cope with the rapid implementation of AI systems without adequate regulation and only AI guidelines? How will facial recognition technology fit in the GDPR? The EU provides many interesting initiatives, which could have a positive impact in the long term. However, it seems to foster a slow and soft approach. Citizens need to be able to trust AI in order for it to be developed. To earn this trust, AI will have to respect ethical standards reflecting EU values. Decision-making should be understandable and human-centric, and be delivered on time. Technology doesn't wait.

We live in an extraordinary age. These are times of fundamental changes in our societies, economic well-being, moral and ethical precepts, philosophical and religious perspectives, and human self-knowledge, as well as in our understanding of our place in the universe. Our generation is about to answer crucial questions like: What is the nature of the universe we live in? Will we ever understand the nature of consciousness? Can we save the planet from climate change and destruction? We are privileged to live through this unique transitional moment.

Shaping the digital future

We find ourselves in the middle of the greatest information and communication revolution in human history. The adoption of the Internet has created one of the most disruptive political, cultural, and societal transformations in history.

Since Aristotle, we have tried hard to understand the causes of everything. However, this ideology is fading. Nowadays, we can crunch an enormous amount of information, providing many beneficial insights. The Internet is one of the most powerful and influential inventions ever created. It has become the cornerstone of the evolution of our civilisation.

In their book, *Networked, the New Social Operating System* (2014), Lee Rainie and Barry Wellman note that human societies co-evolve with technology. Large-scale forces in economics, politics, culture, and religion drive social change, and societies change as they embrace new information and communication technologies (ICTs). During the last 25 years, the Internet and digital technology have evolved into universal extensions of people's networked individualism.

In the next decade, the Internet will continue to grow and will become something like electricity. Essential elements, like the Internet of Things (IoT) and AI will drive its evolution. A new study from Juniper Research – a British consulting company which specialises in identifying new high growth market sectors within the digital ecosystem – found that the total number of IoT connections will reach 83 billion by 2024, rising from 35 billion connections in 2020. This represents a growth of 130% over the next four years.

In a report issued in January 2016, the World Bank said that the Internet's technological changes had not improved access to public services or increased economic opportunities, as had been expected. On the contrary, the report warns that Internet innovations stand to widen inequalities and even hasten the hollowing out of middle-class employment. "Digital technologies are spreading rapidly, but digital dividends like growth, jobs, and services, have lagged behind," the Bank said.

Concerns about the impact of new technologies are not new. In 1589, the inventor William Lee applied to Queen Elizabeth I for a patent on a new stocking frame knitting machine. The machine could produce higher quality stockings, but Elizabeth refused, fearing the effects on hand-knitting industries. "Thou aimest high, Mister Lee," she told him, "Consider thou what the invention could do to my poor subjects. It would assuredly bring to them ruin by depriving them of employment, thus making them beggars." Technology is replacing jobs. For example, the USA is manufacturing twice as much as it did in the 1980s with less than a third of the people employed in manufacturing.

Chapter 12

The Dark Side of the Internet

If once you start down the dark path, forever will it dominate your destiny.

— Yoda in Star Wars

In 2018, a high-ranking diplomat of a non-EU country in Brussels asked me if I was interested in joining Steve Bannon's efforts to export his fiery populism to Europe. "It is very kind of you, but I believe that Bannon is a dangerous man," I kindly refused.

Steve Bannon has been the Darth Vader of Emperor Trump. The core of the Star Wars saga has always been the struggle between the Bright Side of the Force and the Dark Side. But while in Star Wars the "good guys" prevail at the end of each story, the reality is different on planet Earth.

Across the world digital communication has permeated almost every aspect of people's lives. It provides an essential case for examining how new technology affects humans' well-being, human rights, and democracy. The question of whether new and social media undermine our well-being is an essential societal concern. From encouraging suicide to giving people an unhealthy addiction to staring at smartphones, digital technology has been accused of doing more harm than good.

There is increasing evidence that the Internet and social media can influence suicide-related behaviour. Social media can be more addictive than cigarettes and alcohol. It has a powerful draw for many people that leads to them checking it all the time without even thinking about it.

Another serious concern is the impact of digital technologies on democracy. According to a new JRC report, the Joint Research Centre of the EC, the democratic foundations of our societies are under pressure from the influence that social media has on our political opinions and behaviours. One of the most critical public concerns is the use of the Internet as a multiplier of disinformation and manipulation of public opinion in changing people's political behaviour. Armies of trolls, bots, fake social media accounts, "news" websites and online publications are used to spread propaganda, confusion, and fear among innocent people.

Even Tim Berners-Lee, the inventor of the World Wide Web, wrote in his regular birthday letter (2018) that "the web that many connected to years ago is not what new users will find today".

> "What was once a rich selection of blogs and websites has been compressed under the powerful weight of a few dominant platforms. This concentration of power creates a new set of gatekeepers, allowing a handful of platforms to control which ideas and opinions are seen and shared," he added.

In 2018, the revelation that 50 million people had their Facebook profiles harvested by data firm Cambridge Analytica so it could target them with political ads, was a massive blow to the social network. Fundamental questions arise about Facebook's approach to data protection and disclosure. Can the social network adequately secure our most personal data? And if that data is misused, is our democracy still safe?

For example, Brazil's new president makes Trump look like a saint: he praises dictators and wants to destroy the Amazon. Bolsonaro's supporters used fake accounts to flood social media with toxic lies designed to confuse voters and create distrust. Polls show that a large majority of his voters believed these lies, for example, that his opponent was a paedophile.

While most countries use their troll armies to police and influence their own citizens, some have already turned against the EU, the US, and Western-type democracies in general. A 2017 Oxford study noted at least 30 nations were utilising them.

Here are some of the leading public opinion manipulators:

Russia

Moscow is financing legions of pro-Russia Internet bots and trolls. According to internal documents released by a group of hackers in 2013, the Internet Research Agency in St Petersburg employed more than 600 people across Russia. They had an annual budget of $10 million, half of which was paid out in cash. In January 2017, a joint report by the CIA, FBI, and NSA confirmed that there had been Russian interference in the 2016 election. According to this document, the Kremlin's objective was to undermine Americans' confidence in their electoral system and denigrate Hillary Clinton.

Between January 2015 and August 2017, Facebook linked 80,000 publications to the Internet Research Agency through more than 470 different accounts. At the same time, a total of 50,258 Twitter accounts were linked to Russian bots. Those fake accounts were programmed to share false information during the 2016 election period. Approximately 80% of these bots behaved in a way that supported Donald Trump, mostly using the hashtags #donaldtrump, #trump2016, #neverhillary and #trumppence16.

Russia is also trying to discredit the EU and expose it as a failed project. In its EUvsDisinfo database, the European External Action Service outlines different cases of fake stories related to the coronavirus that stemmed from Russian media outlets, such as the "prediction" that the pandemic will cause the collapse of the Schengen Area, the paralysis of the EU, etc.

EUvsDisinfois the flagship project of the EEAS' East StratCom Task Force. It was established in 2015 to better forecast, address, and respond to the Russian Federation's ongoing disinformation campaigns affecting the EU, its member states, and countries in the shared neighbourhood.

EUvsDisinfo's core objective is to increase public awareness and understanding of the Kremlin's disinformation operations, and to help citizens in Europe and beyond develop resistance to digital information and media manipulation.

China

On 10 June 2020, China and Russia were once more accused by the European Union of running disinformation campaigns inside the EU. "Foreign actors and certain third countries, in particular Russia and China, have engaged in targeted influence operations and disinformation campaigns around COVID-19 in the EU, its neighbourhood, and globally, seeking to undermine democratic debate and exacerbate social polarisation, and improve their own image in the COVID-19 context," a communication of the European Commission stated.

The naming of China as a creator of disinformation followed a public scandal in the EEAS. The EU's foreign affairs department denied media reports that it toned down allegations made against China as part of a report into state-led disinformation campaigns, following pressure from Beijing.

Coordinated and covert attempts by China-linked actors to manipulate information –particularly regarding COVID-19, have also been detected in countries including the USA, Argentina, Serbia, Italy, and Taiwan, with the relevant content often delivered in local languages. The online army of Chinese trolls is called the "50-Cent Party", because it is believed they get paid $0.50 per comment that they post. This means that they are eager to get into an argument with you. The more you argue, the more money they make. According to one Harvard study, this group of Internet mercenaries is made up of at least two million people.

Pro-Beijing actors are carrying out a whole range of clandestine activities in different countries and languages. The campaigns aim to spread proven falsehoods, sow societal discord, and panic, manipulate public opinion perceptions, or undermine the democratic process. Evidence revealed last year indicated that some Chinese-language campaigns had begun on platforms like Twitter as early as April 2017. Still the latest round of incidents and investigations points to a more definitive shift in Chinese influence operations.

Turkey

Turkey's ruling party AKP began recruiting a team of 6,000 social media operatives back in 2015. "We aim at developing a positive political language which we are teaching to our volunteers," a party official told the Wall Street Journal (16.09.2013) a few years earlier. "And when the opposing camp spreads disinformation about the party, we correct them with valid information, always using positive language." However, interference by AK trolls has proved not so friendly and they spread false stories.

Turkish trolls deploy three aspects of AKPs populism: serving the people, seducing people, and demonising opponents. Whereas trolls traditionally target and mock institutions, Turkey's political trolls act on behalf of the Islamic establishment. They produce a digital culture of lynching and censorship. Trolls' language is also used by pro-government journalists who work like trolls and attack journalists, academics, and artists critical to the government.

Dissidents are being forced to leave Turkey due to online threats. On some occasions, online abuse has escalated into physical violence. Barbaros Sansal, an LGBT activist, and one of Turkey's most famous fashion designers, said he had been beaten up by pro-Erdogan supporters, including an attack in 2012 which left him with a broken nose. I have been in contact with Mr Sansal during this year and, he told me that he was forced to leave the country in September because of life threats. I was worried when

I saw that his Twitter account with more than half a million followers had disappeared. I received a message later from someone saying that "he posted a tweet mocking the earthquake in Izmir and then shut down his account because of the reactions".

In December 2016, Turkish dissident journalist Abdullah Bozkurt was falsely linked to the assassin of Russian Ambassador Andrei Karlov. The diplomat was killed in an art gallery in Ankara by a Turkish police officer in what is supposed to be the most secure part of Turkey's capital city. A false claim stating that the killer stayed in his apartment was picked up by the government's trolls and disseminated on Twitter. The same journalist describes a Turkish government disinformation campaign with fake stories planted in the media that were subsequently exposed in court in 2020.

In June 2020, Twitter closed 7,340 Turkish accounts for violating its policies. Twitter reported that these accounts were found to be linked to the youth activities of the Justice and Development Party (AKP). The statement said:

> "Based on our analysis of the network's technical indicators and account behaviours, the collection of fake and compromised accounts was being used to amplify political narratives favourable to the AKP, and demonstrated strong support for President Erdogan. We are disclosing 7,340 accounts to the archive today."

Twitter declared that the research on the identification of these accounts was done in conjunction with the Australian Strategy Policy Institute (ASPI) and the Stanford Internet Observatory (SIO).

The Internet is among a few things that humans have built but don't really understand. It is the largest experiment involving anarchy in history – a source for potentially dreadful evil but also tremendous good. We are only just beginning to witness its impact.

Combating fake news

According to the March 2018 Eurobarometer on fake news and online disinformation, 85% of EU citizens perceive fake news as a problem in their country; 83% perceive it as a problem for democracy in general; and 73% are concerned about disinformation online during pre-election periods.

"Fake news" was Collins Dictionary's official Word of the Year for 2017. However, fake news is nothing new. It has been causing mass hysteria, harm, and even death since as far back as the 13th century BC when Ramses spread lies and propaganda that described the Battle of Kadesh as a remarkable victory for the Egyptians. We can even blame fabrications for why in 30 BC, Marc Antony ultimately killed himself when false news of Cleopatra's suicide reached him.

Procopius, a Byzantine historian of the 6th century AD, produced dubious information, known as "Anecdota", which he kept secret until his death, to smear the reputation of Emperor Justinian while praising the emperor in his official histories.

Moreover, according to Joseph Goebbels, Adolf Hitler's propaganda minister in Nazi Germany, if you tell a lie big enough and keep repeating it, people will eventually come to believe it. Just look at what happened in the UK during the Brexit debate.

Fake news plagues us today more than ever with the deliberate spread of misinformation upsetting elections and political decisions. Facebook, the largest social network on the planet, has to answer to increased concerns over its users' spread of hate speech and propaganda.

In March 2018, the newspapers *The Observer* and *The New York Times* alleged that Facebook had known that Cambridge Analytica collected millions of its users' profile data over two years. The data were used without users' consent to influence the Leave campaign in the Brexit referendum and Donald Trump's election in 2016. In September 2019, researchers at Oxford University in the UK found that governments worldwide are stepping up their online disinformation campaigns despite more aggressive regulatory efforts by Internet platforms and governments.

The number of countries with political disinformation campaigns increased to 70 in the last two years, with evidence of social media manipulation by at least one political party or government entity in each nation. Facebook remains the most popular social network for disinformation, hosting organised propaganda campaigns in 56 countries.

Furthermore, Brittany Kaiser, former business development director of Cambridge Analytica, claimed this company interfered in the elections of "at least" 68 countries – adding that the latest general election in Britain in December 2019 included many of the same disinformation tactics seen during the UK's vote in 2016.

> "Technology has advanced greatly in the past few years, and there's now not just one Cambridge Analytica. There are hundreds. They are companies specialising in propaganda as a service, that use fake accounts and bots to spread disinformation and fuel hatred and violence," she added.

During the preparations for elections in the United States, France, and Italy, the influence of international networks spreading false information to steer the voters became apparent. At the same time, an increasing number of organisations are trying to find ways to debunk fake news and ensure the transparency of the information used in political communication. Alexandre Alaphilippe, of the EU DisinfoLab, said during the 2018 Eurocom Conference in Brussels that citizens were not ready for the vast diversity of techniques being used by the people who spread fake information, in part because they evolved so quickly. There was thus a need for many different forms of expertise in all the fields affected by disinformation. EU DisinfoLab is an independent NGO focused on researching and tackling sophisticated disinformation campaigns targeting the EU, its member states, core institutions, and core values.

In a message marking World Communications Day (24.01.2018), Pope Francis denounced fake news, of which he had also been a victim:

> "The difficulty of unmasking and eliminating fake news is due also to the fact that many people interact in homogeneous digital environments impervious to differing perspectives and opinions. *Disinformation* thus thrives on the absence of healthy confrontation with other sources of information that could effectively challenge prejudices and generate constructive dialogue; instead, it risks turning people into unwilling accomplices in spreading biased and baseless ideas."

Not to be confused with satire or parody, fake news intends to damage an entity to gain socially, financially, or politically. It has become a worldwide phenomenon, spreading through social media platforms and fake websites that often imitate credible news sources.

There are numerous examples of companies facing online speculations. In 2017, misleading tweets in which Starbucks was giving away free products to "undocumented" migrants in the US went viral. Advertisements, including the company's logo and pictures of drinks, were circulated with the hashtag #borderfreecoffee. Starbucks denied the event, replying to individuals on Twitter that it was "completely false" and that people had been "completely misinformed".

In January 2019, a video appeared on the Internet showing a Tesla self-driving vehicle hitting a robot prototype at CES, a consumer electronics show in the US attended by international tech reporters. The video went viral, with media outlets running headlines claiming "Self-driving Tesla car kills robot". The video was fake. Tesla does not have a self-driving model, and the robot that was "killed" was, in fact, part of a publicity stunt made by the Russian company that developed it. Yet the incident drew international attention and Tesla's shares fell.

In May 2019, shares in the UK's Metro Bank plunged 11% before it could shake off inaccurate social media rumours that it was facing financial difficulties. Customers queued to access safety deposit boxes.

The rapid spread of fake news shows the power of social platforms to damage reputations and illustrates how corporations are having to be more vigilant and creative in responding.

According to estimates from the University of Southern California and Indiana University, up to 15% of active Twitter users are automated social media accounts, or "bots". At 330 million monthly active users, this would mean that nearly 50 million Twitter accounts could be bots. Malicious social media bots can be used for spreading spam, manipulating financial markets, or influencing elections.

Chapter 13

The Propaganda Emporium

Repeat a lie often enough and it becomes the truth.

— Joseph Goebbels

In 2016, Facebook, Twitter, and other social media had exposed millions of citizens worldwide to false stories about the role of EU, the UK referendum, and the American elections. BuzzFeed News identified more than 100 pro-Trump websites being managed from a town in the former Yugoslav Republic of Macedonia (FYROM) – now called North Macedonia. The town of Veles has experienced a digital gold rush as locals launched more than 100 US politics websites. These sites have American-sounding domain names such as WorldPoliticus.com, USConservativeToday.com, DonaldTrumpNews.com, and USADailyPolitics.com. They published aggressively pro-Trump content aimed at conservatives and Trump supporters in the US. The reasons for launching these sites were purely financial, according to the owners.

With 2.7 billion monthly active users in November 2020, Facebook is the market leader for social networking sites. It drives gigantic traffic and attention to news but fails dismally in the field of civic information. Facebook has become a global vehicle of misinformation. Some of it is driven by ideology, but most is driven by the economic incentive structure Facebook has created. Facebook should care more about the veracity of the news that its users share. When it connects with a Facebook user's personal opinion or sense of identity, the fake news spreads like fire.

In July 2016, the fake website *WTOE 5 News* reported that Pope Francis had broken with tradition and unequivocally endorsed Donald Trump for President of the US. That never happened, however, on Facebook, the Pope's "endorsement" received more than 960,000 shares. Hiring editors to manage what shows up in Facebook's trending topics section seems an excellent solution to me. This is one of the main channels where misinformation is spread.

Donald Trump is a brilliant disciple of Joseph Goebbels, the chief propagandist of Nazi Germany. During his presidency he made thousands of false or misleading statements. In May 2017 Carole McGranahan of the University of Colorado wrote in the American Ethologist:

> "It has long been a truism that politicians lie, but with the entry
> of Donald Trump into the U.S. political domain, the frequency,
> degree, and impact of lying in politics are now unprecedented.
> Donald Trump is different. By all metrics and counting schemes,
> his lies are off the charts. We simply have not seen such an accom-
> plished and effective liar before in U.S. politics."

To be precise, in the four years he was in the White House, Trump made
30,573 false or misleading claims, according to the *Washington Post.*
(https://www.washingtonpost.com/graphics/politics/trump-claims-
database/)

> "We also built the greatest economy in the history of the world…
> Powered by these policies, we built the greatest economy in the
> history of the world."

This is Trump's favourite false claim, so there should be no surprise he
said it twice in his farewell address. By just about any key measure in the
modern era, Dwight D. Eisenhower, Lyndon B. Johnson, and Bill Clinton
presided over more robust economic growth than Trump. The gross domestic product (GDP) grew at an annual rate of 2.3% in 2019, slipping
from 2.9% in 2018 and 2.4% in 2017.

However, in 1997, 1998, and 1999, GDP grew 4.5%, 4.5%, and 4.7%,
respectively. Yet even that period paled in comparison with the post-war
boom in the 1950s or the 1960s. Growth between 1962 and 1966 ranged
from 4.4 to 6.6%. In 1950 and 1951, it was 8.7% and 8%, respectively.
Meanwhile, the unemployment rate reached a low of 3.5% under Trump,
but it dipped as low as 2.5% in 1953.

After the negative impact of the coronavirus crisis on the economy, Trump
jacked up his claim even more, falsely saying it had been the most outstanding economy in the history of the world. Trump used a variation of
this line 493 times, meaning he said it on average every other day.

> "We also got tax cuts, the largest tax cut, and reform in the history
> of our country, by far."

This is Trump's second favourite falsehood, and his remarks at his departure ceremony at Andrews Air Force base mark the 296th time he said it. Even before Trump's tax cut was crafted, he promised it would be the biggest in US history – bigger than Ronald Reagan's 1981 tax cut. Reagan's tax cut amounted to 2.9% of GDP and none of the proposals under consideration came close to that level. Yet Trump persisted in this fiction even when the tax cut was eventually crafted to be the equivalent of 0.9% of GDP, making it the eighth largest tax cut in 100 years.

Examples of dissemination of fake news can also be found in the coverage concerning the 2016 UK referendum on EU membership. Anti-EU media such as *The Sun, Daily Mail, Daily Telegraph*, and *Daily Express* misled their readers by publishing fear-provoking articles based on lies concerning the Turkish accession, the contribution to the EU budget, and the creation of an EU army.

The Brexit campaign even made fake videos by including a woman's scream and smashing glass in footage of a fight between the ruling AK Party and pro-Kurdish politicians in the Turkish Parliament (*The Independent*, 20.06.2016). The video was used to warn of the prospect of Turkey joining the EU. It was uploaded on YouTube and has been used by many quality media outlets globally including Associated Press. The scream sounds very much like a stock sound effect called "Screams6 WomanPanic PE134001" that can be found on the audiomicro.com website.

Social media platforms should hire (more) professional journalists to separate the fake news from the mainstream and inform users about what is fabricated and what is true. However, fake news is not restricted to social media. It is all over the Internet. People should think twice and check the credibility of sources of information before sharing. There are sites such as snopes.com which have a database of known fake stories that is regularly updated. Essentially, be critical when you read online content.

The continued rise of personalised social media feeds and content are hollowing out reporting jobs. Digital media are becoming more critical every day. However, the Internet is full of examples of fake news, misrepresentation, and hate speech that would be unacceptable in print. The press is facing a dual crisis: economic and digital. Digital brought changes in ICT and made technology cheaper and more powerful. It changed business processes and bolstered innovation across all sectors of the economy, including traditional industries. Blogs, citizens journalism, and social media are cheap new media channels that a few years ago didn't exist. This new form of generating news has also created new issues concerning the future of press independence, quality, and transparency.

A journalist's job is to tell a community about itself. Journalists are paid by quality publications to do this job making them economically independent of special interests. Many digital outlets do not have a separation between news and comment or between authentic citizens' contributions and paid content. The decline of newspaper's circulation and the loss of advertising incomes are responsible for critical reorganisation.

Urgent need for regulation

The question of whether the Internet and social media undermine our well-being is an essential societal concern. How many times have you checked your Twitter today? According to a 2016 study of research firm D-scout the typical mobile phone user touches his/her phone 2,617 times a day.

While the Internet has created opportunity, given marginalised groups a voice, and made our daily lives easier, it has also created an opportunity for scammers, given a voice to those who spread hatred, and made all kinds of crime easier to commit.

According to Tim Berners-Lee, the inventor of the World Wide Web, there are three sources of dysfunction affecting today's Internet:

- Deliberate and malicious intent, such as state-sponsored hacking and attacks, criminal behaviour, and online harassment – e.g. Russia, China, Turkey.
- System design that creates perverse incentives where user value is sacrificed, such as ad-based revenue models that commercially reward clickbait and the viral spread of misinformation – e.g. Facebook.
- Unintended negative consequences of benevolent design, such as the outraged and polarised tone and quality of online discourse – e.g. cyberbullying, addictive use, trolling, online witch hunts, fake news, privacy abuse, and suicides.

While the first category is impossible to eradicate, we can create laws to minimise this behaviour, just as we have always done offline. The second category also requires regulation and redesigning systems to change incentives, while the third category calls for research to understand existing systems and possibly model new ones or modify those we already have.

McLuhan's "The medium is the message" theory shows that the manner in which a message is communicated is greatly influenced by the channel that is being employed. The audience's response will depend not only on what is being said but also from which medium it is being delivered.

The impact of social media on democracy and as multiplier of disinformation and manipulation of public opinion is a serious concern. Our relationship with social media in particular has changed our behavioural patterns, destroyed our confidence, and fractured our attention ability. Social media giants have been accused of facilitating illegitimate interference with democratic political processes around the world. Part of this problem has been caused by automated fake accounts passing as humans – malicious bots. Tech giants such as Google, Facebook, and Twitter have been under scrutiny for failing to stop illegitimate interferences with democratic processes on their platforms. These involve different attempts at manipulating public opinion, including malicious bots.

According to a new study published in September 2020 by Cambridge University, radical right anti-EU parties benefit most from fake accounts and malicious bots, to then gain real followers on the back of fake ones. The study identified significant and substantive following of radical right politicians in Europe by malicious bots. Using a large purge of such bots by Twitter in July 2018, researchers found that belonging to an extreme right party is associated with an average loss of up to 5% of an MP's followers within that week, particularly among the most popular and louder anti-EU alt-right politicians. These findings are the first evidence that radical right parties benefit more than other parties from social media bots to inflate their popularity. Thus they artificially get more attention than they should. This has implications for how the EU continues to tackle online abuses and misinformation and for journalists who use Twitter popularity as a source, which might lead to giving radical right parties more attention than they deserve.

The digital world needs new rules, transparency, and accountability. It is the duty of governments to make laws and regulations for the digital age. Governments have a responsibility to protect people's rights and freedoms online. We need open web champions within governments who will act when private sector interests threaten the public good and who will stand up to protect the open Internet.

At pivotal moments, governments in the past have worked together for a better future. With the Universal Declaration of Human Rights, diverse groups of people have been able to agree on essential principles. With the Law of Sea and the Outer Space Treaty, we have preserved new frontiers for the common good. Now too, as the Internet reshapes our world, we have a responsibility to make sure that it is recognised as a human right and that it is built for the public good.

However, in addition to the legal frame for fair information practices and consumer data protection set by governmental regulators, it is crucial for the industry to put meaningful self-regulatory guidelines in place based on a thorough understanding and how they will impact consumers, the economy, and society.

Therefore I believe that the Code of Practice on Disinformation to address the spread of online disinformation and fake news, and the EU Code of Conduct – to prevent hate speech online – are great initiatives of the European Commission and should be signed with tech companies such as Twitter, Facebook, and Google.

Chapter 14

The Brexit Madness

Brexit was a fantastic example of a nation shooting itself full in the face.

— Hugh Grant

Northern Ireland has been a significant obstacle to the Brexit deal. It is clear that what has been negotiated does not work and shows just another aspect of the Brexit madness. In order to avoid a hard border between Ireland and Northern Ireland, the British region remains part of the United Kingdom and, at the same time, part of the EU internal market and the customs union.

This is a paradox which means that nothing can get from the British mainland to the Irish island; which has necessitated a crisis meeting between the EU and the British and caused frustration and anger to swell in Northern Ireland.

The Brexit negotiations focus was the fear that a hard border between the Republic of Ireland and Northern Ireland could cause the conflict to break out again. This is how the current border agreement was made and is a paradox that does not work. It could even lead to new "Troubles" between Catholics and Protestants. There is a real risk that the Northern Ireland Protocol will collapse. The consequences would be inestimable. On the one hand, the whole trade deal with the EU would be in jeopardy; on the other hand, the Good Friday Agreement could break down. The only conceivable alternative to the current construct is a hard border between Ireland and Northern Ireland, and it is possible that this will fuel conflict between Catholics and Protestants, because in the Good Friday Agreement London undertook to keep this border with the Republic of Ireland open and porous.

According to Jane Morrice, former Vice President of the EESC – who was born in Belfast and covered the conflict as BBC reporter:

> "The solution could be relatively simple. By extending the NI Protocol to Scotland, which also voted to remain in the EU, the border would move from the Irish Sea to the less contentious line between Scotland and England. Scotland would be offered the same deal as Northern Ireland and the new "Celtic Protocol"

would allow for the free flow of goods between Scotland, Ireland, and Northern Ireland, similar to the Benelux countries which set up the EU. Above all, this would help remove contentious barriers brought about by Brexit and protect the peace process in Ireland."

"If Brexit was bad for Britain, it was even worse for Northern Ireland. By keeping NI in the EU as part of the UK, the NI Protocol was the compromise to accommodate the majority who voted to remain in the EU and to avoid a hard border on the island of Ireland. Instead, the NI Protocol involved checks at ports between Great Britain and NI but this has caused problems in unionist communities who see a border in the Irish Sea as cutting them adrift from their UK homeland," she added.

In the aftermath of the EU referendum much ink has been spilt in an attempt to explain the outcome and why people voted as they did. I have a vivid memory of Thursday 23 June 2016. Brexit Day. I was walking down the Rue Froissart after a morning event about EU media which had been organised at the Brussels Press Club. UK's departure from the EU was imminent and official confirmation was expected later that night.

I was working on a media relations project for a Dublin-based American communications company that had developed a pan-European "sentiment poll" about the British referendum. The question was simple: "Should the UK leave the EU?" Participants could answer yes or no. The poll was available in all European countries and all official languages of the EU. UK citizens, as well as citizens from other European countries, could vote.

Most polls showed that the UK Leave campaign was taking the lead in the EU referendum. I entered the newspaper shop at the Schuman Roundabout corner and bought all copies of *L'Echo* they had. My article "Brexit ou la communication du mensonge" – Brexit and the communication of lying – was published that day. The lady behind the counter asked me my opinion of the British referendum.

"They will leave the EU," I answered without hesitation.

"And what will happen to the stock markets?" asked a man in the shop.

"They will fall but will stabilise sometime after," I replied.

While the gentleman wondered when the stock markets would stabilise, I left the shop, and went to my office. Brexit was the third significant failure of the EU in a row after the euro and the refugee crises. A few days before, Labour MP Jo Cox had been shot and stabbed to death in the UK by a man shouting "Britain first".

It was the tragic apotheosis of an unprecedented and highly intense campaign that crossed the boundaries of freedom of expression. What should have been a campaign based on political communication degenerated into forecasts of doom and gloom, culminating in lies, drama, hollow rhetoric and ultimately an assassination.

The murder of Jo Cox

"I felt as though I was at a friend's funeral," Vaira Vike-Freiberga, the former president of Latvia, said in an interview after Britain's vote to leave the EU on 23 June 2016. "This is no longer the European Union that we joined." A few days before, Labour MP Jo Cox had been shot dead by a man shouting "Britain First". Both "Stronger In" and "Vote Leave" camps suspended campaigning following the incident for a few days. It was the tragic apotheosis of an unprecedented and extremely intense campaign that crossed the boundaries of freedom of expression.

The Leave campaign engaged the public by using the power of narrative. Feelings of national pride were triggered by presenting a historical record in which Britain was portrayed as a tremendous and influential country – a narrative in the same style as Donald Trump's, "Let's make America great again". Those who wanted to leave argued that by becoming part of the

EU, London had been limited in its greatness as an extraordinary nation. According to this narrative, a Leave vote would set the British free, allowing Britain to become great again.

Vote Leave ran a campaign of misinformation and propaganda to scare voters into quitting the EU. "London sends 350 million pounds every week to Brussels", "London always get bossed around by Brussels", and "Turkey will join the EU in 2020", were the most misleading messages. Brexit leaders assured the electorate it would reclaim the supposed £350 million that Brussels received each week. They knew it was a lie.

When experts declared that the UK would face a £40 billion hole in their public finances, Brexiteers knew how to fight back. They said that the truth-tellers were corrupt liars in Brussels' pocket. Before the referendum, they declared that leaving the EU would reduce immigrant arrivals. After the referendum, they admitted that the number of foreigners coming in would not fall in all probability.

Brexit supporters warned that if Turkey were allowed to join, free movement rules within the EU would see many of their citizens seeking work in the UK which could lead to a five million increase in the population by 2030. Nobody in Europe knows when and if Turkey will ever become a member of the EU. Despite being told that their facts were inexact, those who wanted to leave persisted in advocating disinformation and misleading propaganda on many issues, from migration to the EU payments.

The Remain camp used the element of danger in case of leaving. "Leaving Europe would threaten our economic and our national security," said Prime Minister David Cameron. A group of the UK's most eminent academics indicated that leaving would encourage politicians to pull apart decades of environmental policy established through the EU. "Being in the EU has allowed us to implement legal frameworks that have improved our quality of life, including the air we breathe, the seas we fish in, and have protected the wildlife which crosses national boundaries," they argued.

Weeks after the referendum and despite the super-patriotic tone of the winning Leave campaign, no plans were published in the press on the future of Great Britain by Johnson, Gove, or Farage. Vote Leave did not know how to resolve difficulties with illegal immigration, the National Health Service, Scotland, Ireland, or other problems.

As Nick Cohen wrote in *The Guardian*,

> "Politicians, including Remain politicians, lie, as do the rest of us. But not since the Anglo-French invasion of Suez has the nation's fate been decided by politicians who knowingly made a straight, shameless, incontrovertible lie the first plank of their campaign".

The consequences of the referendum outcome were felt by both British citizens living in Great Britain and millions of British expats living in continental Europe. *Euractiv*, a media platform specialised in EU affairs in Brussels, spoke to a selection of British expats living in Brussels during the weekend after the referendum of 23 June. All strongly supported Remain and some are considering applying for citizenship in other EU countries. A European Commission official, speaking anonymously, said, "People are really upset. Some tears were shed; some people were crying. It has really hit people hard, both Brits and non-Brits". After the UK's decision to leave the EU European institutions sent reassuring emails to EU officials of British nationality, telling them not to worry about their jobs just yet.

Some of the voters who were in favour of London leaving the EU have revealed their regret over the choice after the referendum results were made public. Twitter was full of regretful posts by some of them. One person said: "I personally voted Leave believing these lies, and I regret it more than anything. I feel genuinely robbed of my vote".

I do not think that Boris Johnson believed what he was saying to the people. The following day during the press conference, the expression on his face of a naughty boy astonished by the terror of victory proved it. He didn't think that the Leave campaign would win. He joined it because it served his own interests to become prime minister.

At the time, the question was how the EU should react to the British people's decision to leave the Union?

According to Professor Paul De Grauwe, of the London School of Economics, commenting on his blog, the EU was also responsible for what happened in the UK.

> "The starting point in trying to answer this question [how to react] is the observation that the European Union has a very negative image today, not only in the UK but also in other parts of the EU, leading to dissatisfaction about the European project. I will argue that this dissatisfaction has to do with the inability of the EU to set up a mechanism that protects the losers of globalisation. Worse, the EU has reduced the capacity of national governments to take on the role of protector, while little has been done to create such a mechanism at the EU-level."

> "The problem of the European Union today is that, instead of helping those who suffer from globalisation, it has set up policies that hurt these people even more. It is no surprise that the losers revolt. If the EU continues with austerity and structural reforms, revolt will spread, and will take the form of attempts to exit the Union. It is time the European Union takes the side of the losers of globalisation instead of pushing for policies that mainly benefit the winners," he added.

De Grauwe proposed two solutions. The first is to stop imposing structural reforms on the member states. The second is to boost public investment, which suffered severe collateral damage from the austerity programmes imposed by the EU institutions.

The vice president of the European Commission Frans Timmermans declared that he was not surprised by Britain's vote to leave the EU and called on European leaders to take responsibility for decisions made in Brussels and stop blaming European institutions. Timmermans said buck-passing was a large part of the problem. "Do you constantly say that everything in Brussels is not decided by us, or do you say: I sit at the table in Brussels and I am partly responsible for what has been decided," Timmermans declared during an interview on *NOS TV*'s programme, "Nieuwsuur".

European Union leaders must respond to the UK's vote to leave the EU, by doing more to defend the EU project and its vision. To make it more transparent, social, and responsive to citizens' concerns. This was the key message that came out of Parliament's debate on the British referendum results (05.07.2016) with European Council President Donald Tusk and European Commission President Jean-Claude Juncker.

The Brexit referendum has shown that the people do not trust their representatives anymore and indicates a massive deficit of leadership throughout Europe and worldwide. While politicians differ from one another, genuinely visionary leaders recognise the real issues and make clear, quick, and confident decisions to prevent any ambiguity or confusion. True leaders have to stay humble, inspire trust, and recognise that they still have much to learn. They need to have emotional commitment, curiosity, insight, engagement, and determination. European political leaders should be able to master complexity, orchestrate creativity, and grow emotional commitment.

I have heard many opinions in favour of and against the EU, both before and after the referendum. I believe that leaving the EU was a big mistake which will harm London and the rest of Europe. Great Britain had a lead role to play in Europe and by leaving, it looks as though it refuses to take up its responsibilities. Being part of a market of 500 million is significant for such a vital economy and its people. Many companies invested in the

UK because it was part of the European Union; now many are developing a continental Europe presence instead of a UK presence.

A kind of disappointment was detected after the referendum. According to the *New Zealand Herald,* this country's authorities have registered a massive increase in interest from British citizens wanting to move to New Zealand since the referendum. Only 49 days after the vote, there were 10,647 registrations from the UK compared with 4,599 over the same period in 2015.

Rick Ridder, the former US presidential campaign manager of Howard Dean in 2004, and senior consultant for five other presidential campaigns – Barack Obama, Hilary Clinton, Bill Bradley, Bill Clinton, and Gary Hart – who I interviewed for my book *Rebranding Europe,* believes that the biggest mistake about Brexit was that the UK government actually thought that people would follow those politicians who favoured staying in the EU.

> "The Stay-side failed to communicate that the benefits of staying were much more important than the negatives of getting out. They also forgot that initiatives in referendums are precisely the vehicles that voters use to send their disenchantment with government and express their dissatisfaction. There are many by-elections, special elections where you have voters come out and where they say: look, we don't like the direction and we vote for the other party. Referendums are very similar. They want to send a message to the government," he said.

> "You had David Cameron, Nick Clegg and Jeremy Corbyn, who was somewhat for and somewhat against Brexit. But they kept putting up politicians, and then they tried to use sports stars. I do not care if David Beckham is for or against it. The politicians seemed to think that it was important. Nobody wakes up in the morning and says: Boy, I'm going to vote to stay because David

Beckham thinks it is a good idea. I might buy a different type of soccer ball if David Beckham thinks it's a good idea. It was stupid. You don't start a referendum because politicians want it. You start a referendum because citizens want it. Their inability to gauge citizen's desire for change ultimately caught up with them," he added.

Chapter 15

Being Silent Is a Mistake

Our lives begin to end the day we become silent about things that matter.

— Martin Luther King, Jr.

A few weeks before the European elections of May 2019, the president of the European Commission Jean-Claude Juncker said that he regrets not intervening in the Brexit referendum. The EU could have "destroyed the lies" that led to Britain voting to leave the EU, he said. Speaking at a press conference, Juncker said that David Cameron, UK's prime minister at the time, asked him not to interfere in the referendum campaign. It was a mistake to be silent at such a crucial moment, added the Commission president.

Sometimes, intervention from outside can be counterproductive though. US President Obama declared during his visit to London in April 2016 – only two months before the referendum – that its membership of the EU amplified the power of the UK. He warned it would go "back to the queue" in any trade deal with the US if the country chose to leave the EU.

Although Obama stated that his opinion about Brexit was "part of being friends and being honest", many British experienced it as an intervention in a domestic campaign. At that moment, David Cameron did not see any foreign interference. Instead, he told the UK citizens to listen to the advice of their friends. So why did he ask Juncker not to interfere, and why did Juncker interfere in 2015 to keep Greece inside the euro area yet not in Britain in 2016?

Canadian philosopher Marshall McLuhan's famous claim that "the medium is the message" means that the form of a medium embeds itself in the message, creating a symbiotic relationship by which the medium influences how the message is perceived. But it is more than that. To have an impact, every message needs a face. Every campaign message is personal. In 2016, the debate on Brexit focused mainly on the opinions of the most powerful big business. Later, both camps understood that the referendum would significantly impact the everyday lives of the people. Both campaigns learned to attract human faces, making their cases more personal. When people feel connected to the issue, they feel motivated to vote. Nigel Farage is the face of Brexit. Remain does not have a face. David Cameron, Theresa May, and Jeremy Corbyn failed.

Not challenging the Farage message that Brexit would help fix the UK makes the Conservatives and Labour as responsible for his success as the man himself. There is a straightforward reason for Farage's victory: he was facing no resistance. Silence is the worst strategy you can have in a time of crisis. If you don't clearly communicate your position in a battle, you will be the loser. This was the case in 2016 and it is the case now. It is the problem of all pro-Europeans on the whole continent: pro-Europeans did not have a plan.

The Brexit Party won the most votes in the EU election of 23 May 2019 and received 29 seats in the European Parliament. This was the United Kingdom's final participation in a European Parliament election before leaving the European Union on 31 January 2020.

The president of France, Macron, is right, and the other EU leaders are wrong. Repeatedly extending the Brexit process has reduced Europe's ability to fix itself. Convinced Europeans would be saddened by the finding that a large number of young people in different EU countries had little or no interest in the European election campaign. Overall results, however, confirmed the latest projections, with the centre-right EPP (Christian Democrats) losing ground but remaining the biggest political group with 180 seats, followed by the centre-left S&D (Socialists) with 146 seats.

The first two political groups lost a total of 77 seats. If EPP and S&D lost seats, the Liberals (ALDE) managed to get significant gains, moving from 76 to 109 seats and becoming the third biggest group in the European Parliament. The same applies to the Greens, who went from 57 to 69 seats thanks to historic performances in Germany and France.

After the EU elections, there is now a strong representation of anti-European forces in the Parliament and the populist nightmare will probably not end with Brexit. Although populist, Eurosceptic parties across Europe saw gains, they were less than what some pre-election polls had predicted.

Sixteen years after the last major enlargement with the countries of Central and Eastern Europe the vision of an ever closer union has lost its shine. The movement for less Europe may have already begun. Therefore, being silent is a mistake, but not voting is a bigger one.

Here are some lessons to be learned from the campaigns in favour and against the EU:

(a) Clarity is key

There was a lot of internal fighting in the UK's Leave campaign concerning who should run the campaign and what should come after an exit. The arguments of those who wanted to leave were not clear concerning what the day after would look like. While it was argued that it would bring more freedom for the UK to trade and thus growth to its economy, there were no substantial visions on what that means. At the UN referendum of 2004 for the reunification of Cyprus, also known as the Annan plan, citizens had to vote for draft legislation, which had been negotiated into its final form only a month before the vote. Nothing was clear. People voted on the base of their sentiment and rejected the plan, as even Cyprus legislators did not have enough time to read the whole text. Fear had overtaken everything.

(b) The message needs a face

Every message needs a face to have an impact. Every campaign message is personal. The debate on Brexit focused mainly on the opinions of the most powerful and big business. Both camps then understood that the referendum would significantly impact people's everyday lives and both campaigns attracted human faces to make the message more personal. People felt connected to the issue and motivated to vote.

(c) Keep humanism and dignity

The murder of Labour MP Jo Cox, a mother of two, by a far-right extremist was not only tragic for the UK. It was a tragedy for the whole civilised world and an attack on democracy. One thing that makes our democracy work is the willingness of politicians and members of parliament to meet their voters openly. A democracy conducted behind severe security measures would be pretty fractured and impoverished. Her murder is a sad example of how populism can divide and poison relations between people. More than ever, we need to support quality and independent journalism and scrutinise and challenge myths and populism. More than ever, politicians should stay ethical, honest, and polite in all their communications. They should demonstrate decency and commitment towards the people. The media should create transparency by making important things clear and relevant to citizens. Messages need to be coherent, lucid, concrete, free from jargon and pathos, and connected to real human needs.

(d) We can't take a yes or no vote for granted – including the polls

At the French referendum on the European Constitution held in 2005, the French rejected the treaty. Initial opinion polls showed a clear majority in favour of the constitution, but public opposition grew over time. A few days before the referendum, the *Yes* campaign's lead became smaller than the opinion poll's margin of error. The *No* votes in the Irish referendums on the Treaties of Nice (2001) and Lisbon (2008) demonstrated that a consensus between government and opposition leaders is not always sufficient. In both referendums, the polls predicted a vote in favour of the treaties, but the Irish voted against. Before the 23rd of June, most polls showed the UK Leave campaign taking the lead in the EU referendum.

(e) Tackle propaganda and close the information gap with citizens

We live in a time where citizens are bombarded with information and where every question can be answered by a simple Google search. In such a world how do we get people to remain interested and well informed about the world around them? In the aftermath of the June 2016 EU referendum in the UK, it appeared that there was a widespread lack of information among British voters on the main facts about the EU.

The Leave camp leaders took advantage of this and managed to campaign using, among other methods, lies, propaganda, manipulated information, and false arguments. They were supported by a wide range of tabloids with a large circulation like the *Daily Mail, The Daily Telegraph*, and *The Sun.*

On 16 June 2016, *The Sun* urged everyone to vote for leaving the EU:

> "We urge our readers to beLEAVE in Britain and vote to quit the EU on June 23. This is our last chance to remove ourselves from the undemocratic Brussels machine, and it's time to take it. We must set ourselves free from dictatorial Brussels. Throughout our 43-year membership of the European Union it has proved increasingly greedy, wasteful, bullying, and breathtakingly incompetent in a crisis. Next Thursday, at the ballot box, we can correct this huge and historic mistake. It is our last chance. Because, in no doubt, our future looks far bleaker if we stay in."

Tabloids like *The Sun* never told the ordinary British reader, how the EU had secured peace in Europe or had managed to create a system to ensure the food independence of the continent. Of course newspapers like the *Financial Times* and *The Guardian* backed the Remain campaign, but their circulation is relatively small. The lack of reliable and trustworthy EU information in large parts of the British population was due to the yellow press and the insufficient communication both from London and Brussels itself.

If we look at the figures of Eurobarometer Nr. 83 of May 2015 about how informed UK citizens are about the EU, we can conclude that they are at the very bottom of the ranking. Respondents were asked to say whether each of the following simple statements was true or false: "The EU currently consists of 28 Member States"; "The Members of the European Parliament are directly elected by the citizens of each Member State"; "Switzerland is a Member State of the EU". Unsurprisingly many British started Googling what the EU is, just hours after they voted to leave it.

The bashing enterprise in Great Britain began decades ago when the tabloids adopted an anti-European discourse. Anything that could was blamed on the actions of an apparently "arrogant, crazy and incomprehensible Brussels bureaucracy". If there existed something like an "Anti-EU" press school, the British tabloids would be considered its founders. From the 1980s onwards fictions were created about EU decisions. That editors could get away with such decadent propaganda demonstrates a democratic deficit in Great Britain concerning media.

In its report on the UK published on 4 October 2016, the European Commission against Racism and Intolerance (ECRI) of the Council of Europe describes how tabloid newspapers and the considerable intolerant political discourse on immigration have contributed to an increase in xenophobic sentiment.

British authorities should find a way to establish an independent press regulator according to the recommendations set out in the Leveson Report, a public judicial inquiry into the culture, practices, and ethics of the British press following the *News International* phone hacking scandal. It recommends more rigorous training for journalists to ensure better compliance with ethical standards. It further urges the authorities to sign and ratify the Additional Protocol to the Convention on Cybercrime.

Finally, one of the most important lessons of Brexit is that the process of leaving the EU is the same as the process of accession but vice versa.

Negotiations of each chapter of the "acquis Communautaire" are held chapter by chapter. Some are manageable and some are complex. From this deconstruction process, the EU has gained impressions in terms of technical preparation and safeguarding its acquis.

Killing Erasmus

After four and a half years of negotiations, the EU and the UK finally announced on Thursday, 24 December 2020, Christmas Eve, that they had managed to agree on the terms of their future cooperation and a free trade agreement. We all followed the long and painful process of detachment that for many Europeans was incomprehensible. Some interpreted it as the decline of a country we had learned to admire and choose as the most popular destination for study, work, or tourism.

The Brexit withdrawal deal contains new rules for how the EU and UK will live, work, and trade together. Further to this, British PM Boris Johnson has announced that the UK will not continue to participate in the EU Erasmus programme, allowing hundreds of thousands of students to study at some of Europe's top learning institutions. It will be replaced with a new scheme named after the mathematician Alan Turing.

Many British youth and European academics regret the end of Erasmus. Scottish leader Nicola Sturgeon even spoke of "cultural vandalism". Only students at universities in Northern Ireland will continue to participate in Erasmus as part of an arrangement with the Irish government. But why did the UK PM kill Erasmus for students? A year ago, he promised in the House of Commons that the Erasmus scheme was safe in his hands.

The Erasmus programme supports education, training, youth, and sport in Europe. In 2017, the programme turned 30 years and evolved into Erasmus+. It now provides opportunities for people of all ages and a wide range of organisations.

It favours exchanges between university students and academic personnel, enabling them to study and be trained in other European countries and develop a feeling of understanding for the different kinds of cultures on the continent. It is about sharing cultures, learning language, and each other's habits and ways of living. However, it is much more than that.

Erasmus is probably the most important flagship EU programme for European integration as it supports the creation of a European public sphere and a common identity. It was launched in June 1987, the year that I graduated from the University of Brussels. I am a little bit disappointed because it was not introduced earlier so that I could participate myself. However, I am delighted that my children had the privilege to participate.

Today, Erasmus is one of the most successful projects for shaping European cohesion and should be more developed in the future. It is probably one of the key instruments to support a better connection between European citizens, a shared identity, and more acceptance for a united Europe.

It is the best guarantee for peace and the future of the continent. The programme is named after the Dutch philosopher Erasmus (1469–1536), a self-proclaimed "citizen of the world". He was an opponent of dogmatism, who lived and worked in many places in Europe to expand his knowledge and gain new insights. He also shaped popular culture. His dictionary rescued phrases such as "breaking the ice", "teaching an old dog new tricks", and "leaving no stone unturned" from obscurity.

For more than 30 years, the EU has funded the Erasmus programme. It has enabled over three million European students to spend part of their studies at another higher education institution or an organisation in Europe.

According to the former Education, Culture, Multilingualism and Youth EU Commissioner, Androula Vassiliou, Erasmus is unique because it creates real Europeans. In my interview with her for my book *Rebranding Europe* back in 2017, she declared:

> "Honestly, I have not come across a person who has been an Erasmus beneficiary and who is not a pro-European. I see it with Heads of State. Former Italian PM Matteo Renzi is an Erasmus beneficiary. Also, the PM of Luxembourg Xavier Bettel and former EU Commissioner Cecilia Malmström as well. Erasmus makes you really feel European. You send young people abroad, and they get to know new people, new cultures, they meet their future colleagues from all over Europe. They get the feeling and they get the real sense of communication, of cooperation of understanding which are the real values of Europe."

That is the reason that Boris Johnson killed Erasmus. Like a vampire's fear for the cross, Johnson is afraid of a common European identity and common European values leading to the United States of Europe – a real European Union.

Erasmus brings opportunities to students, staff, trainees, teachers, volunteers, and more. It is not just about Europe or Europeans either — with Erasmus, people from all over the world can access opportunities. The so-called Erasmus generation learns to face the challenges and the potential of the international dimension. The program helps participants to develop a global vision indispensable in every job, profession, or business activity.

Thanks to Erasmus, we now have the first truly European generation. And it is thanks to Erasmus and other programmes like Comenius, Leonardo, and Grundtvig, that the EU has created a Europe of knowledge and is providing a response to the major challenges of our time: to promote lifelong learning, encourage access to education for everybody, and help people acquire recognised qualifications and skills.

The main benefit of the Brexit withdrawal agreement of 24 December 2020 is that trust between the EU and the UK doesn't further deteriorate. It is a good start for all future negotiations. It is no coincidence that the Commission President, Ursula von der Leyen, said that "Europe again sees the UK as a reliable partner". Nothing more than that.

Chapter 16

EU and US: Children of the Same Mother

Nothing in life is to be feared, it is only to be understood. Now is the time to understand more, so that we may fear less.

— Marie Curie

With Joe Biden's victory in US elections, there is at least a four-year win-dow to revive "an alliance of democracies", face up to authoritarian powers and closed economies that exploit the openness on which American and European societies are built, and shape those parts of multilateralism that serve transatlantic interests. EU–US relations are a top priority for the EU's policy debate in 2021, and stakeholders on both sides of the Atlantic are already shaping their strategies.

At the end of January 2021, EU foreign policy chief Josep Borrell and Biden's newly installed Secretary of State Antony Blinken discussed future EU–US relations. They emphasised that transatlantic relations are enter-ing a new chapter. The two discussed "ways to repair, revitalise, and raise the level of ambition in the US–EU relationship", with Blinken thank-ing Borrell for "the EU's leadership in recent years," according to a State Department statement.

Tackling global warming, managing globalisation, building peace, disman-tling inequality and racism, and reinstalling multilateralism, and world-wide cooperation are, I believe, top priorities for the future. Nevertheless, it is the climate that deserves our very first extensive attention. The EU and the US have a significant role to play in saving the planet.

Both North American and EU leaders should develop a base for more and better cooperation and future unification of the EU with the US and Canada. First as a confederation and then as a genuine Union of the West.

Many of us may want to consign 2020 to the dustbin of history. It gave us vital lessons and set the stage for the years to come. It showed us that a global pandemic is not only a health crisis, but also an economic crisis, an education crisis, an inequality crisis, a social crisis, and so much more. We saw rising food insecurity, growing polarisation, and surging mistrust of public institutions and leaders.

We experienced a devastating and disproportionate toll on minorities, women, girls, and marginalised communities. We saw new divisions arise in the world: between young and older people, between people in good health and bad health, between small businesses and big corporations, between more educated and less educated people.

The pandemic has exposed and deepened systematic inequality both within and between countries. It has demonstrated how national interests prevail over international cooperation. The response to the global pandemic has been undermined by some political leaders who have ruthlessly exploited the crisis and weaponised COVID-19 to launch new attacks on human rights.

At the same time, we have seen extraordinary generosity and compassion during this crisis and solidarity across countries and communities. This crisis has shown that humanity finds inspiring ways of synergy when faced with substantial shared challenges. A new spirit of international cooperation might even resolve long-standing conflicts over issues as thorny as the taxation of multinationals in a globalised world, a cause the Biden administration is now taking up.

It looks like some countries adapted better than expected to lockdowns and social distancing in the second wave of the virus than the first. Households and businesses have learned to work more effectively from home, shop online, and experience leisure in a digital form.

However, the pandemic, millions of deaths, social distancing and the resulting economic recession have negatively affected the mental health of many citizens and created new barriers for those already suffering from mental illness and substance use disorders. According to Alison Abbott in *Nature*, researchers worldwide are investigating the causes and impacts of this stress, and some fear that the deterioration in mental health could linger long after the pandemic has subsided.

The European Union

It is too early to assess the political repercussions of the corona pandemic in Europe. Still, decisions taken since February 2020 will have a profound impact. EU leaders have failed in communicating a shared vision, taking a real political commitment to reassure European citizens that the EU is there for them. Different European countries have taken a national approach, focusing less on solidarity and coordination.

It looked as if the corona crisis could be the final nail in the European project's coffin. The "biggest crisis since the EU was founded", said German Chancellor Angela Merkel in early April 2020. During the same year, export bans on urgently needed medical supplies and unilateral border closures gave the sense that "my country first" approaches had destroyed any remaining solidarity between member states.

Nevertheless, European cohesion has come about to an unprecedented degree over the last five years due to Brexit. The EU has ultimately responded in a more or less effective way to the crisis, agreeing on recovery funds for the hardest-hit member states. However, the coronavirus will either kill or cure the EU.

Just two weeks after the Joint Declaration on the Conference on the Future of Europe was signed in Brussels by the European Parliament President David Sassoli, Portuguese Prime Minister António Costa – on behalf of the Presidency of the Council – and by Commission President Ursula von der Leyen, the Executive Board of the Conference on the Future of Europe held its constitutive meeting on 24 March 2021 in Brussels.

The purpose of the Conference was to establish how to give citizens a more significant role in shaping the Union's future policies and ambitions, improving its resilience. The three institutions will organise a series of actions where citizens would have the chance to express their views on the issues that matter to them. The Conference was an opportunity to underpin the democratic legitimacy and functioning of the European project. The aim was to discuss and collect views from EU citizens on matters about the Union which are of interest; whether it is the EU's Health Union, the Green Deal, digital transition, or the way European elections should be held. Those views will dictate the Conference's reform recommendations and hopefully define a sustainable future vision for a more united and effective continent.

At the beginning of the 2000s, the EU seemed to be a tremendous experiment in shared sovereignty that had banished war from Europe. The EU was perceived as the only equitably prosperous and rule-of-law-respecting superpower, even without the military determination to play global policeman. Many believed that its unique combination of open borders, integrated markets and democratic institutions made Europe's "soft power" equal to the "hard power of the US".

The EU received the Peace Nobel Prize in 2012 for preventing European countries from declaring war on each other in the past 60 years. However, Europe is perceived as being always too late and too slow. In their Lisbon Strategy (2000–10), the development plan for the EU economy, European leaders declared their aim of becoming the most competitive and dynamic knowledge-based economy in the world. However, these high-minded words have not been accompanied by the structural reforms necessary for creating stable growth in the long term and for dynamic response to globalisation.

The EU has to be united and speak with one voice if it wants to play any significant role on the planet. European citizens should understand that the relatively small countries that constitute the EU are no longer able to face the major global challenges on their own. European countries are now so interconnected that issues like the regulation of financial markets, research, and innovation investment, national security, economic recovery plans, or the fight against climate change should be dealt with as a Union.

The world is not going to wait for Europe to make up its mind. The EU must show leadership through its efforts to solve the current worldwide problems. It needs a system of governance with a better balance between efficiency and democratic legitimacy. The EU needs to reinvent itself. Indeed, today's environment does not seem to ideal for new ambitions or grand ideas. Nevertheless, a solution-driven Union can only strengthen its legitimacy if its policies and successes are communicated clearly and comprehensively to the citizens.

Europe needs to develop a stronger identity and a common public sphere. The European identity consists of a set of values shared by all EU citizens. Nowadays, the EU is characterised by two opposing trends. One emphasises the importance of national identities and the right to difference. The other advocates the right to a collective identity and to a cosmopolitan culture. These two trends do not necessarily exclude each other. A united Europe does not mean the extinction of national identities. It respects the right to difference and diversity while being cosmopolitan.

Jürgen Habermas, one of the most influential sociologists and philosophers of the 20th century, said that the public sphere encourages rational will-formation. This is a sphere of sound and democratic social interaction. During the 19th century, the project of creating a *United States of Europe* gained support among European intellectuals. Several political leaders were convinced that a closer union between European States could not be based only on governments and their administrations. A peaceful union of states had to be sustained by a rapprochement between European nations and their citizens. This perspective was frequently promoted inside many European networks of societies, clubs, associations, and academics.

Moreover, today the active involvement of civil society could be of tremendous support in the formation of a European public sphere. Civil society has grown in size and influence. Nowadays, mobile information and communication technology are becoming highly relevant methods to connect and obtain social change. The lines between communication and advocacy are not very clear anymore. Citizen-centred campaigns powered by digital and social media can drive social movements and achieve political change.

A European public sphere is extremely relevant for the future of EU integration because it influences the quality of democracy in the EU. A democratic Union requires that public discourse and discussion of issues are dealt with at EU level. Without a public sphere, institutional reforms of the EU that seek to make it more democratic are doomed to fail.

The role of the media is paramount in developing a common identity and a public sphere. However, freedom of expression in relation to governance is not always easy to summarise – with debates reaching back millennia. As Francis Fukuyama document in his book *The Origins of Political Order* (2011), Emperor Qin – the founder of the first unified Chinese state in the third century BC – saw control of ideas as fundamental to his state building project.

> "If such conditions are not prohibited, the Imperial power will decline above, and partisanships will form below," wrote Li Si, Qin's Chancellor, in 213 BC. "It is expedient that these be prohibited. Your servant requests that all persons possessing works of literature, the Shijing (Book of Odes), the Shu (the Book of History) and the discussions of the various philosophers should destroy them."

Four hundred Confucian scholars who resisted were reportedly buried alive.

Two millennia later, the extreme opposite approach to state building was articulated by Thomas Jefferson in his famous quote, "If I had to choose between government without newspapers, or newspapers without a government, I should not hesitate a moment to prefer the latter".

The increase of Eurosceptic and nationalist parties in Europe, populism, the Brexit and the antipathy towards institutions and politics, in general, are all alarms for immediate action. In France, they make the difference between a *marriage d' amour* and a *marriage de raison*. The relationship between Great Britain and the EU has always been a *marriage de raison* – and so it is with Hungary and Poland. These kinds of relationships are actually those that last the least.

However, Brexit may turn the tide towards more cohesion in Europe. In particular, during periods of constant change that which we are currently experiencing, random events shape history. Stimulating the engagement of the people and restoring the public's approval to the EU are enormous political challenges. Nevertheless, crises can only be resolved if there is a sustainable support and joint effort by members of the EU at national, regional, and local levels.

The EU is being criticised not only from the inside. Over the last years many negative articles have appeared on the future of Europe. According to a specific press, the EU is not inspirational anymore and is on the brink of collapse. A systematic policy of *divide and rule* has been pursued by neoconservatives in the US, nationalists in Russia, and other countries like China and Turkey. Europe is suffering from an incoherent structure and lacks a sustainable vision.

While Europe is the most inspiring political and economic experiment in the world, it does not have a face. The EU is completely faceless, while at the same time, it confuses the planet with so many titles and functions. In the US you have Joe Biden, who is the president of the country. In Russia, you have Vladimir Putin, who is the president there. In the EU we have the president of the Commission, the president of the European Parliament and the president of the Council. "Who are you? I have never heard of you. Nobody in Europe has ever heard of you". That is what the British ultra nationalist and troublemaker, Nigel Farage, asked Herman

Van Rompuy, the first EU Council president in February 2010, who had just made his first speech to members of the European Parliament since being appointed by EU leaders to the newly-created top job.

The EU is perceived as irrelevant and people do not understand what is happening in Brussels. There is long-running confusion about the European institutions, about who speaks for the EU and its policies. The Union also fails to deliver when it comes to communication at the national, regional, European, and global level. One of the main challenges for communicating Europe is relaying the message that the EU is not a threat to national sovereignty. However, the problem is structural and there is an urgent need for institutional reform.

If the policies are not good and not in the public interest, then they must be adjusted. The EU has to change its policies and restructure the way it functions. The best strategy to choose for a new structure is to go back to the basics and proceed with what the founding fathers of the EU had in mind: a united Europe with democratically elected institutions, a strong parliament, and one government, with respect for diversity and national identities, and a robust social model.

Most of the politicians are inflexible for the time being and there are no signs that they want to change. Nevertheless, they will have to. The biggest challenge for European legislators is to show that they will be responsive to citizens' needs. Not just the needs of their country and themselves.

It is hard to find still inspiring politicians in Europe like Robert Schuman, Konrad Adenauer, Alcide De Gasperi, Paul-Henri Spaak, and Winston Churchill in our days. In the meantime, public opinion has been hijacked by populists and Eurosceptics pretending that isolationism and closed frontiers will save us from our daily problems.

They capitalise on the growing sense of insecurity among the citizens of Europe, and the growing fear of the unknown. Will dismantling Europe save us from illegal immigration and unemployment? Will it bring more security, more jobs, and less crime? I am not sure about that. On the contrary, I think it will bring more unemployment, poverty, inequality, less security, and most probably armed conflict.

The United States

America is a nation of immigrants, from their very origins. The original sins of decimating the Native Americans and the slavery of Africans were committed by the first immigrants, essentially English, Ulster-Scots, Dutch, and German. Since the 19th century, the country has repeated the same pattern of discrimination then assimilation as each successive group of immigrants arrives and seeks to join the Great American Experiment.

The Irish were the largest immigrant group during the Second Wave of American immigration. About one-third of Ireland's population left home in the 1800s – often as indentured servants, on ships sometimes called "coffin ships", to become unskilled labour or join the Union Army. In the beginning, they were stereotyped as drunkards, fighters, and cheats; but later seen as total contributors to US society as police, firefighters, politicians, and entertainers and ultimately accepted.

As the 19th century progressed into the early 20th century, Jews arrived and Catholics from Italy, Poland, and other European countries like Greece, Hungary, and Russia. They were not always welcome in the more or less Anglo-Saxon society. The surge in immigration led to America's first organised anti-immigrant backlash in the 1850s. Opposition to immigrants was influenced by many differences between the existing US population and the newcomers.

Most Americans were Protestant and strongly prejudiced against the Catholicism of most new immigrants. Many Protestant Americans still saw the Pope as the Antichrist. They viewed Catholics as religious terrorists out to subvert American democracy. Anti-immigration movements arose, from the nativist and anti-Catholic Know-Nothing Party in the 1850s to the Chinese Exclusion Act passed by Congress in 1882.

The size and greater cultural diversity of the Third Wave (1890s–1920s) gave rise toa significant new xenophobia that would slam the door on new arrivals in the 1920s. For example, in the early 20th century, Greeks were discriminated against in many ways. In February of 1909, a major anti-Greek riot took place in South Omaha, Nebraska. The Greek population was forced to leave the city, while properties owned by Greek migrants were destroyed.

On 26 July 1922, in direct response to a "campaign of extermination" orchestrated by the KKK, Greek-American community leaders founded the Order of AHEPA, the American Hellenic Educational Progressive Association in Atlanta, home to the Imperial Palace of the Knights of the Ku Klux Klan. Atlanta anchored the Klan's nationwide anti-Hellenism offensive of the early 1920s, which featured boycotts of Greek merchants amid incidents of anti-Greek violence all over the country.

Since Operation Wetback in 1954, perhaps the dominant challenge for US immigration policy has been the legal and illegal flow of Mexicans, together with a fluctuating and unsteady reaction of welcome and rejection. As a result of these policies, the country has managed to turn immigration, the source of much energy, growth, and innovation into an angry, mean, divisive argument about walls and race.

Trump implemented several hardline immigration policies, including a zero-tolerance policy that separated children from parents who crossed illegally through the US–Mexico border. America's policies towards migrants at the southern border have shifted again as Washington pivoted from former president Donald Trump's rigid immigration views to President Joe Biden's less restrictive position.

A massive pandemic, climate change, racism, immigration, societal division, gun control, reforming the voting system: Joe Biden, the new American president faces multiple Herculean tasks. Nevertheless, he could determine American politics for decades and consolidate US world leadership. He would be an unexpected hero if he succeeds, and an easy target if he fails. His job is extremely difficult.

A few weeks before taking his oath on 20 January 2020, a rebellion was directed by his predecessor Donald Trump. At first the usual festive display could not continue because of COVID-19, so a virtual event was organised. However, the risk of future rebellions and violence has been added to the democratic process. Just as if it were 1861 when Abraham Lincoln was brought to Washington in disguise because of fear of an attack.

Trump falsely claimed that the election was stolen and rigged, repeating that message to millions of followers. Conservative media amplified that in the lead-up to the violence of 6 January that was intended to stop the ceremonial counting of the Electoral College votes from the states that showed Joe Biden had won the presidential election.

The challenges are enormous. The US is a country deeply divided by two viruses: COVID-19 and Trumpism. During the primaries, Biden was seen as a boring centre candidate, a ghost from the past, a career politician with no vision. Slowly but surely, he has moved on, under the pressure of the circumstances. The last 12 months have been extremely complicated. COVID-19, Black Lives Matter and Donald Trump's rebellion have put even more urgent work on the agenda than the new president could have imagined.

The last four years have tested US democracy and highlighted divisions. Nevertheless, the seeds for what happened on 6 January, the violence that left five dead at the Capitol, have been sown for longer.

"We have many, many people who have been radicalised by constant lies about everything, the virus, and our institutions, but especially about the lies about the election", former FBI Director James Comey said on MSNBC. "And among that group of people who have been deluded are people who have been moved to violence almost in the way that Al Qaeda motivates its foot soldiers with a constant stream of lies telling them you're on the Lord's side. Some people think they are on the right side of history because of the president," he added.

Propaganda and disinformation news streams have led to radicalisation on the right. Most people think that radicalisation takes place in dark corners of the Internet, but it has been happening under the bright lights of prime-time cable news, through shared Facebook memes and Internet links that tell you what you want to believe, and through a president who has touted false conspiracies and demonised the media.

The US alt-right has changed since the emergence of the Tea Party movement. The domestic threats that have come to the fore in recent months have long been in the making. They precede Trump's refusal to accept his re-election loss and his encouragement of supporters – including right-wing armed groups – to attack the Capitol.

Intensified by political polarisation and Trump, right-wing armed groups have been mobilising and gaining an increased sense of impunity since the 1990s. They are now capitalising on the economic difficulties and political unrest associated with the corona pandemic.

Right-wing armed groups in the United States include a variety of white supremacist, anti-immigrant, anti-federal-government, pro-gun-ownership, and survivalist groups who envision a civil war in the country. The so-called "accelerationists" (whose aim is to trigger unprecedented revolt and establish new, unique political and economic systems) and the boogaloo movement (which has also been described as a militia) seek to advance it.

These varied movements are separate from each other but sometimes intermesh, a trend that was accelerated during the Trump presidency. Some individuals are members of multiple groups at the same time, while rejecting others. The number and membership in right-wing armed groups increased when Barack Obama was elected president, with their recruits outraged by the election of a biracial president with a liberal agenda.

Unravelling that will be difficult and presents a serious challenge to President Biden, who has made *unity* a central message. Biden also presented an ambitious COVID-plan, and he will probably need Republicans to be on board to get it through.

It will be more difficult because Trump unscrupulously led millions of his followers to believe that wearing masks was not entirely necessary and that the US was "rounding the corner" on the coronavirus pandemic when in fact it has only worsened.

When Gerald Ford became president in 1974, in the wake of Richard Nixon's resignation due to the Watergate scandal, he announced: "Our long national nightmare is over". For many, the inauguration of President Biden is a "déjà vu". Another national nightmare has been brought down by still-functioning and vital elements of US democracy, especially the judiciary, a free press, and foreign affairs.

For example, any attempt by Donald Trump to improve relations with Russia was doomed from the start. Having been compromised by Moscow's interference in the 2016 presidential election, Trump could not afford to be seen as supporting Russian interests, especially in a number of key areas. Meanwhile, Congress was not only unwilling to lift sanctions on Russia but added to them after the Russian interference was exposed.

In his inauguration speech, Biden laid out a vision that reflects both boldness and pragmatism. He expressed his deep commitment to servant leadership, saying that his "whole soul is in it". He called on everyone in the country to live up to its highest aspirations by coming together in unity. By centering moral leadership, truth, justice, possibility, and courage, the new president delivered the message the country needed to hear to join together and respond to problems from now on.

Nevertheless, the priority of the new government is the corona war. Since he took office, Biden's team has attacked the problem on multiple fronts. They have unleashed billions of dollars to boost vaccinations and testing and developed a model to deploy more than 10,000 active-duty troops to join even more National Guard members to vaccinate people.

Chapter 17

The Union of the West

L'utopie est la vérité de demain.

— Victor Hugo

Over the past two decades, Russia and China have defined their country's interests in ways that are incompatible those of the EU and the US. The latter believe that democracy, the rule of law, and the provision of security to the former USSR satellites, Africa, and some Asiatic democracies enhance stability. Moscow and Peking, meanwhile, consider the spread of democracy to be a threat to their regimes and believe that having vulnerable neighbours enhances their security.

The EU and the US are already working together on several international peace and stability projects in countries like Bosnia, Ukraine, and Georgia. They have also contributed to the peace process in Northern Ireland with the Good Friday Agreement. According to Jane Morrice, former Vice President of the European Economic and Social Committee who covered the conflict as BBC reporter, "the United States and the European Union both have a vested interest in maintaining peace and promoting reconciliation in Northern Ireland. The long-standing attachment of America to its Irish roots is fabled in folklore and visible to all."

> "Both the US and the EU have shown remarkable generosity in their support for the people of Northern Ireland. The US invested immense political capital at the highest level supporting the peace process from the very top-down. The EU approach has been different. Operating from the bottom up, the EU supports grassroots communities coming together to enable the peace process to take root under its peace programme. The success of their efforts working alongside the British, Irish, and local communities to bring an end to decades of conflict is legendary, culminating in the Good Friday Agreement," she added.

The Second World War was devastating for the entire planet. Especially in Europe, the human losses were extremely severe, and people were shocked to discover the atrocities perpetrated by Germany's Nazi regime and international fascism. Several European countries' economies were left in tatters. Industrial and agricultural infrastructures had been destroyed, towns and cities razed to the ground by bombing raids, transportation infrastructures badly damaged, and there were chronic food shortages.

When it became less important on the international stage by the emergence of the United States and the Soviet Union as two new superpowers, Western Europe realised that its recovery would come through unity; through the pooling of its economic resources (where necessary with US financial, technical, and military support); and through the creation of jointly run, efficient institutions.

Given the rise in influence of the United States and the Soviet Union and their increasing rivalry, the countries of Europe, exhausted by the global conflict, were faced with three fundamental questions

(a) An economic question: how could material damage be repaired and economic activity revived on the old continent?
(b) A political question: how could they prevent the return of a conflict that had laid the continent and the world to waste?
(c) A cultural question: how could the survival and renaissance of European civilisation be ensured in the face of the increasing threats represented by the ideological schism and confrontation between the victorious US and USSR?

Western Europe hoped to reclaim its place on the international stage by uniting the peoples of Europe. Pro-European movements, some of which originated in the Resistance, moved into action, and vigorously promoted the idea of European unification. The idea of a united Europe, which some elites had already promoted during the interwar period, rapidly gained ground in the wake of the Second World War.

Thousands of young people dreamed of a united Europe, sometimes even of a unified and peaceful world. While reconstruction was an immediate priority in the post-war period, many people advocated the creation of an autonomous European entity. To avoid the world being divided into two antagonistic blocs and to prevent war which would inevitably ensue, it seemed essential to establish a third European pole. In this context, there were calls for Western countries to adopt a neutral stance in the face of American materialism and Soviet totalitarianism. However, non-alignment, which became increasingly difficult to implement as the Cold War intensified, was soon defended only by the pacifist and internationalist movements.

The US and EU have been interacting for more than sixty years. US–EU relations officially started in 1953 when US ambassadors visited the European Coal and Steel Community. The two parties share a good relationship which has been strengthened by cooperation on trade, military defence, and shared values. The challenge for the United States and Europe in the years ahead will be to manage the particular problems confronting them to help rebalance the relationship. The new collaboration should differ this time, moving away from European dependence and American dominance towards a more nearly equal partnership.

Meeting contemporary challenges will not be easy. For Europe, it requires devoting more significant resources and broadening its strategic vision. For America, it means sharing not just burdens but power, responsibility, and authority. With Russia, China, and regional dictatorships like Turkey and Iran getting more confrontational, it is becoming increasingly clear that doing anything less will erode the foundation of the existing alliance both sides of the Atlantic are dedicated to preserving.

EU–US relations should go further than a traditional alliance. It may sound utopic but a closer synergy between Europe and North America – including Canada – would be beneficial for both parties. Europe and North America are children of the same mother. A great Union of the West would be the best guarantee for creating a plausible superstate with one billion citizens. The new Union will protect liberal democracy across the planet and face the future challenges posed to humanity successfully. It will provide leadership in many regions in the world including the Eastern Mediterranean and Libya and will keep Russia and China at bay.

We need a solid and sustainable Union for a viable and secure future tackling issues such as climate change, water pollution, terrorism, ageing, unethical AI, and the protection of minorities and human rights. A Union that is able to ensure ethical and societal values based on freedom, democracy, equality, and press liberty.

Europeans and Americans are closely linked culturally, economically, and through the democratic values they share. A Union of the West would provide peace, prosperity, and security to a billion citizens. It would form the world's biggest marketplace by enabling people to sell products, provide services without any restrictions, and reinforce medium-term growth and development strategies.

This future Union will protect its citizens against the downsides of globalisation by supporting small and medium enterprises – the backbone of world economy – and developing rules to ensure that large multinational corporations pay their fair share of taxes. It will secure lasting peace, stability, and a growing internal market and demand. It will become the strongest economic power in the world. Free trade and removal of non-tariff barriers will help to reduce costs and prices for consumers. Increased trade will create more jobs and higher income.

The multilateral world is in deep crisis. There is growing concern about the fate of this historically reliable system, which was built after the Second World War under US leadership. The erosion of international treaties and regulations – and hence of cooperation at a global level – has been accelerating. The Trump administration pulled the US out of numerous international agreements, including the Intermediate-Range Nuclear Forces Treaty (INF) and the Paris Climate Agreement, just to name a few.

Further to this, China is expanding its global influence, including within multilateral institutions. Breaches of international law, especially by Moscow and Beijing, have been on the rise, along with increased protectionism and isolationism. Fortunately, Joe Biden has been elected as a new US president and this is the first step back to a multilateral order after Trump's "America First" stance.

The differences between US and China seem to have increased in number. The world's two largest economies have been locked in a bitter trade battle. The dispute has seen the US and China impose tariffs on hundreds of billions of dollars' worth of each other's goods. Donald Trump has long accused China of unfair trading practices and intellectual property theft. In China, there is a perception that America is trying to curb its rise as a global economic power. Four years and a new president later, US tariffs on Chinese products remain. The Biden administration has expressed a wish to discuss US–China trade issues with its allies first.

However, on 30 December 2020, the EU and China have concluded in principle the negotiations for a Comprehensive Agreement on Investment (CAI). The EU's specific objectives were to provide for new opportunities and improved conditions for access to the EU and Chinese markets for Chinese and EU investors as well as address critical challenges of the regulatory environment, including those related to transparency and licensing. There has been much criticism of the deal, especially from the US, and as of 30 March 2021, it had not been signed off. In the CAI, the EU sees mostly a business deal, while China sees mostly a strategic win that leaves Washington outside.

As Alicia Garcia-Herrero analyses in the Brussels think tank Bruegel,

> "the deal is important politically as it shows the EU's commitment to its own economic sovereignty without constraints from the US and it follows the example set by the 10 members of the Association of Southeast Asian Nations, Australia, Japan, and

South Korea in signing the Regional Comprehensive Economic Partnership back in November. Suddenly, it looks as if US President-elect Joe Biden has been left alone in his pursuit to contain China even before he is sworn in on Jan. 20".

Nevertheless, the CAI is still a draft and needs to undergo legal review and ratification by the European Parliament and approval by the Council on the EU side to become effective.

The time has come for the United States and Europe to find ways to boost their relationship and seek common, sustainable, and innovative grounds from which to address global shifts and challenges. They already stand very close to each other in sharing similar challenges and worldviews. Together, they form the backbone of the West.

The two powers have a significant long-term successful partnership. They share common interests and values, historical, and political ties and geopolitical reality. Both the US and the EU need to start the conversation about building a new strong Union for a fairer and greener world. A stronger Union of the West in preserving security and peace. Soft Europe and hard America can learn from each other and represent a unique combination of both forms of power.

Acknowledgements

A large part of this book was written during the 2020–21 corona crisis in a beautiful house near the Botanic Garden of Meise, just a few kilometres outside Brussels and on the sunny green island of Corfu.

I would like to express my gratitude to the many people who saw me through this book. To all those who provided support, read, wrote, offered comments, and allowed me to quote them. The completion of t could not have been possible without the participation and assistance of those people. Many thanks as well to the interviewees.

In particular, I would like to thank my sons Straton and Leander, and my wife Helena without whose support, input, and encouragement this book would have been finished many months later. Their contributions are sincerely appreciated and gratefully acknowledged.

Also, I would like to thank Noel Swinnen for his input and critical reflections and Lesley Wyldbore for the editing.

About the Author

With a background including positions such as Communication Officer at the European Commission and Press Officer and Spokesperson to diplomatic missions in Brussels, Stavros Papagianneas is currently the Managing Director of PR consultancy StP Communications and the founder of Steps 4 Europe. This pro-EU non-profit association aims to reinforce the European public sphere and promote the values of the EU.

He is a senior communications leader with more than 25 years' experience in corporate and public communications, public affairs, PR and digital. In 2017, 2018, and 2019, Stavros was named by the pan-European news platform *Euractiv* as one of the TOP 40 EU Influencers and is a public speaker and blogger too.

Stavros has been a member of the Working Party on Information of the Council of the European Union. He is the author of the books: *Rebranding Europe; Powerful Online Communication; Saving Your reputation in the Digital Age* and many articles in EU media such as *Euractiv, New Europe, EU Observer, Euronews, L' Echo, De Tijd, Communication Director, Irish Tech News*, and *Research Europe*.

Stavros is a graduate in Communication Sciences from the University of Brussels and has given lectures in universities across Europe: University of Cantabria, University of Vilnius, University of Brussels (VUB), Institute of European Studies (IES), and Thomas More University.

Twitter: @StPapagianneas

Bibliography

Abbott, Alison, Covid's mental-health toll: how scientists are tracking a surge in depression, Nature, 03.02.2021.

AFP, Trump says to send thousands of troops police to US capital's streets, 02.06.2020.

Alba, D, **Satariano**, A, At least 70 countries have had disinformation campaigns, study finds, New York Times, 26.09.2019.

Ahrend, Daphne, Living, working and COVID-19, Eurofound, 06.11.2020

Albayrak, A, **Parkinson**, J, Turkey's government forms 6,000-member social media team, Wall Street Journal, 01.09.2013.

Alemano, Alberto, European strategic autonomy in 2020, Groupes d' Etudes Géopolitiques, 29.12.2020 https://geopolitique.eu/en/2020/12/29/european-strategic-autonomy-in-2020/

AHVAL NEWS, Erdogan's army of online trolls forcing dissidents to leave Turkey, 18.07.2020.

Applebaum, Anne, Twilight of Democracy: The Seductive Lure of Authoritarianism, Anchor, 2020.

Baker, Peter, For Trump and the nation, a final test of accountability, New York Times, 09.01.2021.

Barber, Tony, The decline of Europe is a global concern, Financial Times, 21.12.2015.

Barnett, Steven, The tragic downfall of British media, Foreign Policy, 08.07.2016.

BBC, Social media firms fail to act on Covid-19 fake news, 04.06.2020 https://www.bbc.com/news/technology-52903680

Begg, Jain, **Draxler**, Juraj, **Mortensen**, Jurgen, Is social Europe fit for globalization, CEPS, January 2007.

Berners-Lee, Tim, The web is under threat. Join us and fight for it, web-foundation.org, 12.03.2018.

Berners-Lee, Tim, 30 years on, what's next #ForTheWeb. webfoundation.org, 12.03.2019.

Boffey, Daniel, Italy criticises EU for being slow to help over coronavirus epidemic, The Guardian, 11.03.2020.

Bozkurt, Abdullah, Turkish government disinformation campaign with fake stories planted in the media exposed in court, Nordic Monitor, 31.09.2020.

Brzozowski, Alexandra, Number of bleach-related incidents up in Belgium due to COVID-19 fears, Euractiv, 20.05.2020.

Brown, Steve, Resilience and Innovation. Lessons from the pandemic, CEOWORLD Magazine, 13.05.2020

Bröning, Michael, The rise of populism in Europe, Foreign Affairs, 03.16.2016.

Brüggeman, Michael, How the EU constructs the European public sphere, Seven strategies for information policy, Journal of the European Institute for Communication and Culture Javnost – The Public, 12(2), pp. 57–74, 2005.

Brusden, Jim, Oliver, Christian, EU failed to heed emissions warning in 2013, Financial Times, 25.10.2015.

Bulut, Egin, **Yoruk**, Erdem, Trolls and political polarisation in Turkey, International Journal of Communication, Vol 11, 2017. 4093-4117.

Calwalladr, Carole, **Harrison**, Graham, Revealed: 50 million Facebook profiles harvested for Cambridge Analytica in major data breach, The Guardian, 17.03.2018.

Camus, Albert, La Peste, Gallimard, 1947.

Carbon Brief, Climate strikers: Open letter to EU leaders on why their new climate law is surrender, 03.03.2020 www.carbonbrief.org

Carbon Brief, How climate change misinformation spreads online, 26.06.2020.

CBS News, Unilever joins Facebook ad boycott over racist content, 26.06.2020.

Castanho Silva, Bruno, **Proksch**, Sven-Oliver, Fake it till you make it. A natural experiment to identify European politician's benefit from Twitter bots, Cambridge University Press, 11.09.2020.

Cathcart, Brian, Don't forget the role of the press in Brexit, Open Democracy UK, 30.07.2016 https://www.opendemocracy.net/uk/brian-cathcart/dont-forget-role-of-press-in-brexit

Chadwich, Vince, **Wakefield** Lawrence, Youth to leaders: Europe's biggest crisis is economic, Politico, 12.08.2016.

Chassany, Anne-Sylvaine, **Foy** Henry & **Atkins** Ralph, Anti-Brussels rhetoric goes mainstream across Europe, The Financial Times, 16.09.2016.

Clegg, Nick, Combating COVID-19 misinformation across our apps, Facebook News, 04.05.2020 https://about.fb.com/news/2020/03/com bating-covid-19-misinformation/

Crew, Sarah, Coronavirus in Belgium. Urgent call for protective equipment donations to nursing homes in Brussels, The Bulletin, 17.04.2020.

Coombs, WT, Impact of past crises on current crisis communication insights from situational crisis communication theory, Journal of Business Communication, 41, pp. 265–289, 2004.

Council of Europe, Freedom of expression and information in times of crisishttps://www.coe.int/en/web/freedom-expression/freedom-of-expression-and-information-in-times-of-crisis

Council of Europe, New handbook on protecting the right to freedom of expression under the European Convention on Human Rights https://www.coe.int/en/web/freedom-expression/home/-/asset_publisher/RAupmF2S6voG/content/new-handbook-on-protecting-the-right-to-freedom-of-expression-under-the-european-convention-on-human-rights

Cohen Nick, There are liars and then there's Boris Johnson and Michael Gove, The Guardian, 25.06.2016.

Cooper Charlie, Vote Leave campaign video "doctored" to include fake screams of woman, The Independent, 20.06.2016. http://www.independent.co.uk/news/uk/politics/eu-referendum-vote-leave-campaign-turkey-video-doctored-screams-a7092191.html

Coy Peter, After Brexit, here's what's next for Europe, Bloomberg, 30.06.2016.

Cuddy, Alice, European Parliament votes to trigger Art. 7 sanctions against Hungary, Euronews, 12.09.2018.

CVCE, The post-war European idea and the first European movements (1945–1949), Luxembourg.

Dale, Daniel, **Subramaniam**, Tara, Fact check: Donald Trump made 115 false claims in the last two weeks of February, CNN Politics, 09.03.2021.

Daily Sabah, AK Party founded new Turkey Digital Office for the general elections, 11.05.2015.

De La Baume, Maia, What is the Conference on the Future of Europe, Politico, 04.03.2021.

Dearnell Adrian, Crisis communications in the age of social media, Forbes, 31.10.2019.

de Botton, Alain, Camus on the coronavirus, New York Times, 19.03.2020.

Deane, James, Media and communication in governance, It is time to rethink, OECD, Paris, 2015.

De la Gazza, Alejandro, How social media is shaping our fears of – and response to the coronavirus, Time, 16.03.2020.

Dietrich, Gini, Spin sucks. Communication and reputation management in the digital age, Pearson, 2014.

Debouté Alexandre, Alliance entre 7 quotidiens leaders en Europe, Le Figaro, 10.03.2015.

De Grauwe Paul, The EU should take the side of the losers of globalization, Ivory Tower, 01.07.2016 http://escoriallaan.blogspot.be/2016/07/the-eu-should-take-side-of-losers-of.html

Dreher Axel, **Gaston** Noel, **Martens** Pim, Measuring globalisation. Gauging its consequences, Springer, 2008

Duarte, Nancy, Good leadership is about communicating why, Harvard Business Review, 06.05.2020

The Economist, Babelicious, Multilingualism at the EU, 30.04.2015.

The Economist, The euro crisis was not a government-debt crisis, 23.11.2015.

Edelman 2020 Trust Barometer, 19.01.2020. https://www.edelman.com/trustbarometer

Edelman 2020 Trust Barometer Spring Update, 05.05.2020. https://www.edelman.com/research/trust-2020-spring-update

Edmonson, Amy, The fearless organisation, Wiley, 2019.

Edmonson, Amy, Don't hide bad news in times of crisis, Harvard Business Review, 06.03.2020.

Edmonson, Catie, Facing backslash, Republicans confront Trump's effect on their party, New York Times, 09.01.2021.

EEAS, Special reports disinformation around the Covid-19 pandemic, EUvsDiSiNFO, March, May & April 2020 https://euvsdisinfo.eu/category/blog/eeas-special-reports/

Egkolfopoulou, M, **Sebenius**, A, Facebook violence curbs thwarted by groups using code words, Bloomberg Technology, 12.05.2020.

Elliot Larry, IMF's own watchdog criticises its handling of eurozone crisis, The Guardian, 28.07.2016.

Este, Jonathan, Russian disinformation in the time of Covid-19, The conversation, 08.07.2020.

Euractiv, Brussels Brits react in horror to Brexit: "What the hell went wrong?", 26.06.2016.

European Policy Strategy Centre, EU's industrial Policy after Siemens, Alstom, Brussels, 18.03.2019.

European Policy Strategy Centre, Rethinking Strategic Autonomy in the Digital Age, July 2019.

European Commission, The Single Market in a changing world, (COM) 772 Final, 22.11.2018.

European Commission, Towards a more efficient and democratic decision making in EU tax policy, (COM 2019) 8 Final, 15.01.2019

European Commission, Further strengthening the Rule of Law within the Union State of play and possible next steps, (COM 2019) 163 Final, 03.04.2019

European Commission, Fighting coronavirus disinformation, 29.04.2020 https://ec.europa.eu/info/sites/info/files/corona_fighting_disinformation.pdf

European Commission, Study for an assessment of the implementation of the Code of Practice on Disinformation, Brussels, May 2020 https://ec.europa.eu/digital-single-market/en/news/study-assessment-implementation-code-practice-disinformation

European Commission, Joint Communication in tackling COVID-19 disinformation, Brussels, 10.06.2020 https://ec.europa.eu/info/sites/info/files/communication-tackling-covid-19-disinformation-getting-facts-right_en.pdf

European Commission, Strategic Plan 2016–2020, DG Communication.

European Parliament, Communicating Europe in Partnership, 22.10.2008. http://www.europarl.europa.eu/pdf/declaration_insti/declaration_final_EN.pdf

European Parliament, Journalism and new media. Creating a public sphere in Europe. Resolution on Journalism and new media, 07.09.2010. (http://www.europarl.europa.eu/sides/getDoc.do?pubRef=-//EP//TEXT+TA+P7-TA-2010-0307+0+DOC+XML+V0//EN)

European Parliament, Coronavirus: EU increases action against disinformation, 22.06.2020. https://www.europarl.europa.eu/news/en/headlines/society/20200618STO81510/coronavirus-eu-increases-action-against-disinformation

European Parliament, Rule of law in Poland and Hungary has worsened, Press Release, 16.01.2020 https://www.europarl.europa.eu/news/en/press-room/20200109IPR69907/rule-of-law-in-poland-and-hungary-has-worsened

EU Agency for Fundamental Rights, What do rights mean for people in the EU. Fundamental rights survey, 24.06.2020 https://fra.europa.eu/en/publication/2020/fundamental-rights-survey-trust

European Ombudsman, Ombudsman calls for "blame Brussels" culture to end, Press Release, 17.01.2019.

EUVSINFO.EU, Disinformation can kill, Issue 19, 26.03.2020 https://euvsdisinfo.eu/disinformation-can-kill/

Farrell David & **Scully** Roger, Representing Europe's Citizens? Electoral Institutionsand the Failure of Parliamentary Representation in the European Union, Oxford, Oxford University Press, 2007.

Fazi, Thomas, How austerity has crippled the European economy in numbers, Social Europe, 31.03.2016.

Felbab-Brown, Vanda, How to counter right-wing armed groups in the US, Brookings, 21.01.21.

Feyen, Benjamin & **Krzaklcwska,** Ewa (eds.) The ERASMUS Phenomenon – Symbol of a New European Generation? Peter Lang Edition, 2013.

Fleming, S, **Peel**, M, **Hopkins**, V, EU identity crisis, Poland, Hungary and the fight over Brussels' values, Financial Times, 04.12.2020.

Forman, R, **Atun**, R, **McKee** M, **Mossialos**, E, 12 lessons learned from the management of coronavirus pandemic, ScienceDirect, 10.05.2020.

Forrest, Adam, Coronavirus: 5G conspiracy theory now most common fake news story surrounding pandemic, The Independent, 21.04.2020.

France 24, Twitter shuts thousands of accounts linked to China, Russia and Turkey, 12.06.2020 https://www.france24.com/en/20200612-twitter-shuts-thousands-of-accounts-linked-to-china-russia-and-turkey

Friedman, Uri, New Zealand's PM may be the most effective leader on the planet. The Atlantic, 19.04.2020 https://www.theatlantic.com/politics/archive/2020/04/jacinda-ardern-new-zealand-leadership-coronavirus/610237/

Fox, Erica, New Zealand PM Jacinda Ardern is the leader we have been waiting for, Forbes, 22.03.2019.

Fu, Beimeng, China's paid Internet trolls aren't who you think they are, BuzzFeed News, 20.05.2016.

Fukuyama Francis, The origins of political order: From prehuman times to the French revolution, Farrar, Straus and Giroux, New York, 2011.

Fukuyama Francis, The pandemic and political order, Foreign Affairs, July 2020.

Garton Ash Timothy, As an English European, this is the biggest defeat of my political life, The Guardian, 24.06.2016.

Gadwalladr, C, **Graham-Harrison**, E, Revealed: 50 million Facebook profiles harvested for Cambridge Analytica in major data breach, The Guardian, 17.03.2018.

Garcia-Herrero, Alicia, Europe's disappointing investment deal with China, Bruegel, 04.01.2021.

Georgalou, Mariza, Small stories of the Greek crisis on Facebook, Social Media and Society, July–December 2015.

German Marshall Fund of the United States, Pan-European Parties in a Time of Resurgent Nationalism, Policy Paper, 16.05.2019

Gilman, Sander, Moral panic and pandemics, The Lancet, 29.05.2010.

Gotev, Georgi, Commission responds to Orban's anti-immigration campaign, Euractiv, 28.02.2019.

Gotev, Georgi, Juncker vows to fight Brussels-bashing before European elections, Euractiv, 23.04.2019.

Gramellini, Massimo, Cara Europa, impara da noila scaltra mossa del cavallo, La Stampa, 26.01.2012.

Habermas, Jürgen, Structural Transformation of the Public Sphere, Polity Press, 1992

Harari, Yuval Noah, The world after coronavirus, Financial Times, 20.03.2020 https://www.ft.com/content/19d90308-6858-11ea-a3c9-1fe6 fedcca75

Harris, John, The Brexit disaster has been brewing in the Conservative party for 30 years, The Guardian, 13.12.2020.

Harris Sarah Ann, Brexit "regretters" say they were not really voting to get out of the EU, The Huffington Post, 27.06.2016.

Hill, Fiona, Yes it was a coup attempt. Here's why, Politico, 11.01.2021.

Horodny, Elena, Europe has a crucial identity crisis, Business Insider UK, 05.01.2016.

Hsu, Tiffany, The brands pulling ads from Facebook over hate speech, New York Times, 26.06.2020.

Illing, Sean, Fareed Zakaria made a scary prediction about democracy in 1997 – and it is coming true, Vox.com, 04.07.2017.

Institute for Strategic Dialogue, COVID-19 disinformation briefing, 27.03.2020 – https://www.isdglobal.org/wp-content/uploads/2020/03/COVID-19-Briefing-Institute-for-Strategic-Dialogue-27th-March-2020.pdf

Irish Times, Prodi exudes optimism on imperative of enlargement, 14.11.2001.

Jefferson, Thomas, Letter from Paris to Edward Carrington, 1787.

Jespen Maria & **Serrano Pascual** Amparo (ed.), Unwrapping the European Social Model, The Policy Press, Bristol, 2006.

Jin, K-X, Keeping people safe and informed about the coronavirus, Facebook News, 04.05.2020 https://about.fb.com/news/2020/07/coronavirus/

Joannin Pascal (publ. dir.), Euroscepticism and Europhobia: the threat of Populism, Foundation Robert Schuman, European Issue 375, 14.12.2015.

Jones, S, **Waters**, L, **Holland**, O, **Belvins**, J, **Iverson**, D, Developing pandemic communication strategies, Journal of Business Research, 02.02.2010, pp. 126–132.

Juarez, Juana, The future of communicating the European Parliament, 25 Years of Public Communication in Europe, Club of Venice 1986–2011, 2011, pp. 91–98.

Karnitschnig, Matthew, Europe to Turkey: We won't be bullied on refugees, Politico, 10.05.2016.

Kemp, Simon, Report: Most important data on digital audiences during coronavirus, The Next Web https://thenextweb.com/growth-quarters/2020/04/24/report-most-important-data-on-digital-audiences-during-coronavirus/

Kimmel, Barbara (ed.), Trust Inc. Strategies for building your company's most valuable asset, Next Decade, 2014.

King, G, **Pan**, J, **Roberts**, M, How the Chinese government fabricates social media posts for strategic distraction, not engaged argument, American Political Science Review (2017) 111(3), 484–501.

Kraus, Peter & **Sciortino,** Giuseppe (eds.), Linking the European Union with the Citizens. Evaluation of the EU's Diversity Policies Aiming to Create an Inclusive European Public Sphere. EUROSPHERE Final Comparative Study, Vol.2, 2013. http://eurospheres.org/files/2010/07/Eurosphere_WP8.2_Final_scientific_deliverable1.pdf

Kuchler, Hannah, Companies scramble to combat fake news, Financial Times, 22.09.2017.

Liu Brooke & **Horsley,** Suzanne, The government communication decision wheel: Toward a public relations model for the public sector, Journal of Public Relations, 19(4), 377–393, 2007.

Lyons Kate, The ten best Euro myths, The Guardian, 23.06.2016.

Martins, Ana Isabel, **Lecheler,** Sophie, **De Vreese,** Claes, Information flow and communication deficit: Perceptions of Brussels-based correspondents and EU officials, European Integration, 34(4), pp. 305–322, June 2012.

Marshall, Arian, A Tesla-robot crash stunt shows we need robocar schooling, Wired, 08.01.2019.

McGranahan, Carole, An anthropology of lying: Trump and the political sociality of moral outrage, American Ethnologist, 27.04.2017.

McLuhan, Marshall, Understanding media: The extensions of Man, McGraw-Hill, New York, 1964.

McManara, Kathleen, The Politics of Everyday Europe: Constructing Authority in the EU, AbeBooks, 2015.

Mecking, Olga, Defining European identity in a divided Europe, Bloomberg, 08.05.2017.

#Media4EU: EU strategy for independent and sustainable media, Fondation Euractiv, 29.01.2015 http://www.euractiv.com/wp-content/uploads/sites/2/2015/01/media4eu-eu-strategy-for-independent-sustainable-media-final-29-01-201.pdf

Meehan, William, Solutions to America's seven biggest problems, Forbes, 14.02.2020.

Merritt, Giles, The EU's Digital Compass is no road map to success, Friends of Europe, 23.03.2021.

Measuring European identity, European Commission, Horizon 2020, 2015. https://ec.europa.eu/programmes/horizon2020/en/news/measuring-european-identity

Miller, Debra, Pandemics, Lucent Press, 2007.

Moran, Carmen, También hay lunes en España, El Pais, 25.01.2012.

Moritz, Michael, Europe should forget Google and investigate its own shortcomings, Financial Times, 22.04.2016.

Naffi, N, **Davidson**, A-L, **Jawhar**, H, 5 ways to stop the "infodemic", the increasing misinformation about the coronavirus, The Conversation, 21.05.2020.

Naftulin, Julia, Here's how many times we touch our phones every day, Business Insider, 13.07.2016.

New York Post, The Post says: Give it up, Mr President – for your sake and the nations', 27.12.2020.

Nossel, Suzanne, Don't let leaders use the coronavirus as an excuse to violate civil liberties, Foreign Policy, 13.04.2020 https://foreignpolicy.com/2020/04/13/governments-coronavirus-pandemic-civil-liberties/

NOS TV, Frans Timmermans: Britten mogen wat mij betreft blijven, NOS Nieuwsuur, 05.07.2016.

Nugent, Neil, The government and politics of the European Union, Palgrave McMillan, 2010.

OECD, A governance practitioner's notebook. Alternative ideas and approaches, Paris, 2015.

Official Journal of the EU, 04.02.2014, EU Regulation, 1295/2013, European Parliament & Council of 11.12.2013 establishing the Creative Europe Programme (2014–2020) http://eur-lex.europa.eu/LexUriServ/LexUriServ.do?uri=OJ:L:2013:347:0221:0237:EN:PDF

Onur, V, **Ferrara**, E, **Davis**, C, **Menczer**, F, **Flammini**, A, Online human-bot interactions, detection, estimation, and characterisation, ICWSM, 2017.

Open Hearing Social Media Influence in the 2016 US Election, Hearing before the Select Committee on Intelligence of the US Senate, One hundred fifteenth Congress First Session, 01.11.2017.

Papadogiannis, Nikolaos, Is there such thing as a European identity? The Conversation, 21.05.2019.

Papagianneas, Leander, A Decade of Pertinent Crisis, StP Communications Blog, 11.05.2020 https://www.stpcommunications.com/post/a-decade-of-pertinent-crisis

Papagianneas, Stavros, The case for re-branding Greece, Communication Director, Issue 3, 2015.

Papagianneas, Stavros, Eurolanden zijn mee verantwoordelijk voor Griekse crisis, De Tijd, 06.02.2015.

Papagianneas, Stavros, What next for research and innovation in Greece, Research Europe, 21.05.2015.

Papagianneas, Stavros, Powerful Online Communication, Bookboon, London, 2016.

Papagianneas, Stavros, L' Europe á bout de souffle, L' Echo, 11.03.2016.

Papagianneas, Stavros, Communicating Brexit, Communication Director, 21.06.2016.

Papagianneas, Stavros, Brexit ou la communication du mensonge, L'Echo, 23.06.2016.

Papagianneas, Stavros, Rebranding Europe, ASP Publishers, Brussels, 2017.

Papagianneas, Stavros, Communication: The weak part of European integration, Euractiv, 05.09.2017 https://www.euractiv.com/section/politics/opinion/communication-the-weak-part-of-european-integration/

Papagianneas, Stavros, Artificial Intelligence: A blessing or a curse?, Irish Tech News, 30.04.2018.

Papagianneas, Stavros, The EU's war against fake news, Communication Director, 11.02.2019.

Papagianneas, Stavros, Saving Your Reputation in the Digital Age, 2020 https://bookboon.com/en/saving-your-reputation-in-the-digital-age-ebook

Papagianneas, Stavros, Core elements of crisis communications strategy, StP Communications Blog, 02.04.2020 https://www.stpcommunications.com/post/core-elements-of-modern-crisis-communications-strategy

Papagianneas, Stavros, Lessons in leadership, Euractiv, 03.04.2020 https://www.euractiv.com/section/future-eu/opinion/lessons-in-leadership-for-eu/1451130/

Papagianneas, Stavros, Communicating the future: The opinion of the experts, StP Communications Blog, 27.04.2020 https://www.stpcommunications.com/post/communicating-the-future-the-opinion-of-the-experts

Papagianneas, Stavros, What future for the Future of Europe Conference, EU Observer, 14.05.2020.

Pen America, Losing the news, The decimation of local journalists and the search for solutions, 20.11.2020.

Pickard, Victor, Journalism's market failure is a crisis for democracy, Harvard Business review, 12.03.2020.

Pope Francis, Message of His Holiness Pope Francis for world communications day, The Truth will set you free (Jn 8:32), Fake news and journalism for peace, 24.01.2018 http://www.vatican.va/content/francesco/en/

messages/communications/documents/papa-francesco_20180124_messaggio-comunicazioni-sociali.html

Porter, Jon, Facebook and Instagram to remove coronavirus misinformation, The Verge, 31.01.2020.

Powell, Alvin, **Walsh**, Coleen, And now the way forward, The Harvard Gazette, 20.01.2021.

Rainie, Lee, **Wellman,** Barry, Networked, The New Social Operating System, The MIT Press, 2014.

Rinaldi David, A new start for social Europe, Notre Europe, Jacques Delors Institute, February 2016.

Rinke, Andreas, Coronavirus pandemic is historical test for EU, Merkel says, Reuters, 06.04.2020.

Risi, Jennifer, How strategic communications can define corporate reputation, PR News, 18.11.2015.

Rolando, Stefano, Thirty years dedicated to a certain idea of Europe, Club of Venice, Belgian State, Chancellery of the PM, November 2016.

Rutenberg, Jim, Media's next challenge: overcoming the threat of fake news, NY Times, 06.11.2016.

Sicakkan, Hakan (ed.), Linking the European Union with the Citizens. Evaluation of the EU's Policies Aiming to Create a Democratic European Public Sphere. EUROSPHERE Final Comparative Study, Vol.1, 2013. (http://eurospheres.org/files/2010/07/Eurosphere_WP8.1_Final_scientific-deliverable3.pdf)

Sicakkan, Hakan, Diversity and the European Public Sphere Towards a Citizens' Europe. EUROSPHERE Final Comparative Study, Vol.3, 2013. (http://eurospheres.org/files/2010/07/EUROSPHERE_Final-Report_Web_version2.pdf)

Schmidt, Eric & **Cohen,** Jared, The New Digital Age, Reshaping the Future of People, Nations and Business, John Murray Publishers, 2014.

Scott, Mark, Russia and China push fake news aimed at weakening Europe report, Politico, 01.04.2020 https://www.politico.eu/article/russia-china-disinformation-coronavirus-covid19-facebook-google/

Silverman Craig, **Alexander** Lawrence, How teens in the Balkans are duping Trump supporters with fake news, BuzzFeed News, 04.11.2016.

Simons, Margaret, Journalism faces a crisis worldwide. We might be entering a new dark age, The Guardian, 15.09.2017.

Spiegel Online, IMF admits major mistakes on Greek bailout, 06.06.2016.

Special Eurobarometer 386, Europeans and their languages report, European Commission, Directorate-General for Education and Culture, Directorate-General for Translation and Directorate-General for Interpretation, Directorate-General for Communication, June 2012.

Stanley-Bekker, Isaac, **Romm**, Tony, Pro-gym activists using Facebook groups to push anti-quarantine protests, Washington Post, 20.04.2020.

Stiglitz, Joseph, The Euro: How a common currency threatens the future of Europe, W.W. Norton and Company, New York, 2016.

Stolton, Samuel, Regulation against fake news very important Reynders says, Euractiv, 15.04.2020 https://www.euractiv.com/section/digital/news/regulation-against-fake-news-very-important-reynders-says/

Stroobants, Jean Pierre, **Ducourtieux,** Cécile, Brexit : colère et frustration à Bruxelles après l'annonce du retrait de Boris Johnson, Le Monde, 02.07.2016.

Tech Transparency Project, Extremists are using Facebook to organise for civil war and coronavirus, 22.04.2020 https://www.techtransparencyproject.org/articles/extremists-are-using-facebook-to-organize-for-civil-war-amid-coronavirus

Truax, Chris, Let's try to protect the 2020 election. Here's how to prove you are not a Russian troll, USA Today, 20.02.2020.

Twitter, Disclosing networks of state-linked information operations we have removed, 12.06.2020.

UN, Pause before sharing, to help stop viral spread of COVID-19 misinformation, 30.06.2020 https://news.un.org/en/story/2020/06/1067422

UNESCO, Journalism, Fake news and disinformation, Handbook for journalism education and training, 2018 https://en.unesco.org/node/301521

Varga, Somogy, The politics of Nation Branding: Collective identity and public sphere in the neoliberal state, Philosophy & Social Criticism, October 2013. 39(8): pp. 825–845.

Varoufakis, Yanis, And the weak suffer what they must? Europe's crisis and America's economic future, The Bodley Head, London, 2016.

Venzon, A, **Cahen-Salvador**, C, **Boeselager**, D, Now is the time to create a real European democracy, Euractiv, 03.05.2019.

Verhofstadt, Guy, Le mal européen, Editions Plon, 2016.

Vigdor, Neil, Conway says the more violence erupts, the better it is for rump's reelection prospects, New York Times, 27.0.2020.

Voxeurop, A map showing how knowledgeable Europeans are about the EU, 29.06.2016.

Warell, Margie, Do people feel you genuinely care? Why empathy is crucial to leading through crisis, Forbes, 13.04.2020.

Walt, Stephen, The collapse of the liberal world order, Foreign Policy, 26.06.2016.

Washington Post, In four years, President Trump made 70,573 false or misleading claims, 20.01.2021.

Wendling, M, The (almost) complete history of fake news, BBC News, 22.01.2018.

Wendling, C, **Radish**, J, **Jacobzone,** S, The use of social media in risk and crisis communication, **OECD**, 2013 https://read.oecd-ilibrary.org/ governance/the-use-of-social-media-in-risk-and-crisis-communication_ 5k3v01fskp9s-en#page1

Wind Marlene, Incompetent political leaders and the media are destroying Europe, Euractiv, 31.05.2016.

Wong E, **Rosenberg**, M, **Barnes**, J, Chinese agents helped spread messages that sowed virus panic in the US, officials say, New York Times, 23.04.2020.

Wood, Vincent, Fake news worse during election campaign than Brexit referendum whistleblower says, The Independent, 27.01.2017.

Zakaria, Fareed, The rise of illiberal democracy, Foreign Affairs, 76(6) Nov-Dec 1997.

Zizek, Slavoj, Pandemic, COVID-19 shakes the world, Polity, New York, 2020.

Interviews

Morrice, Jane, former Vice President of the European Economic and Social Committee (EESC) responsible for communications (2013-2015) and former BBC correspondent.

Merritt, Giles, Founder of Brussels think tank Friends of Europe and former EU correspondent for Financial Times.

Cecchini, Sergio, Director Communication & Fundraising, Médecins Sans Frontières.

Dabbs, Michael, Senior Communications Officer, The Gill Foundation.

Kumar, Abhinav, Chief Marketing & Communications Officer – Global Markets, TATA.

de Bruin, Marijn, Professor Behavioural Medicine and Health Psychology. Corona Behavioural Unit, Dutch National Institute of Health and Environment.

Rolando, Stefano, Professor IULM University Milano, President Club of Venice.

Ricorda, Marco, Former Member for the President of the European Parliament Antonio Tajani, and Communication Officer at the International Centre for Migration Policy Development (ICMPD)

List of Abbreviations

Acquis	Also acquis communautaire. The legal order of the European Union
AHEPA	American Hellenic Educational Progressive Association
AI	Artificial Intelligence
Brexit	United Kingdom's withdrawal from the EU following an advisory referendum held in June 2016
CAI	Comprehensive Agreement Investment EU-China
CFSP	Common Foreign and Security Policy
Citizens' Initiative	Petition allowing one million individuals, who are citizens of at least a quarter of the EU countries, to directly call the European Commission to propose a legal act on specific issues of EU's competence
C-level	Senior management
CoR	Committee of the Regions
EC	European Commission
DG COMM	Directorate-General Communication of the European Commission
ECB	European Central Bank
EEAS	European External Action Service
EESC	European Economic and Social Committee
Erasmus	EU student exchange programme
EP	European Parliament

EU	European Union
EU Council	Summit of presidents and prime ministers of all EU countries
Eurobarometer	Public opinion surveys conducted on behalf of the European Commission
EuroparlTV	European Parliament's web video service
EPSC	European Policy Strategy Centre
GDPR	General Data Protection Regulation
IFJ	International Federation of Journalists
IMF	International Monetary Fund
JRC	Joint Research Centre of the European Commission
LGBT	Lesbian, Gay, Bisexual and Transgender
MEP	Member of the European Parliament
MP	Member of Parliament
OECD	Organisation for Economic Co-operation and Development
Schuman Square	Place in Brussels with a big concentration of EU buildings and services
SME	Small and medium-sized enterprises
Spitzenkandidaten	German word for "top candidates". As part of the EU elections, the European parties can name their candidate for Commission president
UK	United Kingdom
UN	United Nations
US	United States
USSR	Union of Soviet Socialist Republics (Russian: CCCP)